Praise for *Adoption 1*

"Karen Springs draws from a tremendous variety of adoption journeys to paint a remarkably honest and multifaceted picture of what adoption is like in real life. Here is all the sweetness and celebration, sorrow and struggle that adoption includes—often within the very same story."

— JEDD MEDEFIND, president of Christian Alliance for Orphans

"For over a decade of serving in Ukraine, Karen had the opportunity to walk alongside children and families and experience the gift of watching them be joined together through adoption. Fourteen years after beginning her journey, she received another gift—to return to many of those families, hear their stories of joy and challenge, and learn from them. We now have Karen's gift to us—this incredibly insightful book, *Adoption Through the Rearview Mirror*. Throughout this book, Karen deepens our understanding of the needs of adopted children, adoptive parents, and biological siblings, and she teaches us so much more. I highly recommend this book."

—JAYNE SCHOOLER, author of *Wounded Children, Healing Homes* and *Telling the Truth to Your Adopted or Foster Child*

"As a mom to eight young adult daughters, seven through adoption, and a foster care/adoption trainer, I've heard and experienced my fair share of 'rearview mirror' moments. The beautiful expectations that we have of adopting a child who has no family quickly meet the heartbreaking reality of parenting a child who has experienced a complex history of trauma and loss. For too many adoptive families, when glamorized expectations meet sometimes harsh reality, they can fall apart. What Karen has communicated through the pages of *Adoption Through the Review Mirror* should be required reading for every potential adoptive family as full preparation for the beautiful and broken journey that lies before them. Using the stories of real parents who are or have been in the trenches, Karen artfully paints a realistic picture of adoption so that expectant parents can enter the journey more realistically. The old saying goes that if you fail to prepare, you prepare to fail. I'm so grateful for this book, for these stories, and for Karen's faithfulness to capture a realistic picture of adoption. Through it, precious families will succeed and precious children's lives will truly be transformed."

—PAM PARISH, founder and CEO of Connections Homes, author of three devotions for foster and adoptive families: *Ready or Not*, *Battle-Weary Parents*, and *The Gift*

"A refreshingly honest, vulnerable, and empowering book about the adoption journey. With personal stories, real-life accounts from families, and timeless applications, *Adoption Through the Rearview Mirror* is a must-read for anyone involved in the care and advocacy of vulnerable children."

—MIKE AND KRISTIN BERRY, authors of *Honestly Adoption: Answers to 101 Questions About Adoption and Foster Care*

"Karen gives a gift to the adoption community by sharing vulnerably her experiences and the experiences of adoptive families. In a culture primed to put its best foot forward, we are at our best when we share with one another lessons we've learned, and that intention is at the heart of every story contained in this book. I appreciated Karen's mention of spiritual warfare and faith lessons. Helping adoptive families and their children thrive is not just a battle we win with best practice but one that requires us to acknowledge the spiritual fight and the One who has already won. Your family will benefit from all the wisdom shared!"

—BETH GUCKENBERGER, author, speaker, adoptive mother, missionary

"In her remarkable book, *Adoption Through the Rearview Mirror*, author Karen Springs reminds us that adoption is always a journey for an adopted child—and also for the adoptive parents and siblings. This important book is based on Karen's experience assisting hundreds of Americans in their adoption of Ukrainian orphans. . . The stories contained in this book resulting from her reunions with these families and research chronicle the roadmap of adoption, with all its twists and turns. Karen views joys and sorrows through the eternal perspective and insights of Scripture. This book has been a revelation and encouragement to me as an adoptive parent. I wholeheartedly recommend it to parents who have adopted or fostered children—or are considering this step. And to all who care for the millions of children globally who don't have families."

—ANITA DEYNEKA, Board Member at A Family for Every Orphan, Mission Eurasia, and World Without Orphans

Adoption Through the Rearview Mirror

Learning from Stories of Heartache and Hope

Karen Springs

Adoption Through the Rearview Mirror: Learning from Stories of Heartache and Hope
Copyright © 2020 by Karen Springs

Published by Forward Reflections Publishing.

Cover by Honnah Weber
Interior by Galina Schaefer

Any internet addresses, phone numbers, or company or product information printed in this book are offered as a resource and are not intended in any way to be or to imply an endorsement by the author or publisher, nor does either party vouch for the existence, content, or services of these sites, phone numbers, companies, or products beyond the life of this book.

Unless otherwise noted, Scriptures quotations are taken from the Holy Bible, New International Version®, NIV®. Copyright © 1973, 1978, 1984, 2011 by Biblica, Inc.™ Used by permission of Zondervan. All rights reserved worldwide. www.zondervan.com. The "NIV" and "New International Version" are trademarks registered in the United States Patent and Trademark Office by Biblica, Inc.™

Scripture quotations marked ESV are taken from The Holy Bible, English Standard Version® (ESV®). Copyright © 2001 by Crossway, a publishing ministry of Good News Publishers. All rights reserved.

LCCN: 2020908288

ISBN: 978-0-9999014-0-3

Printed in the United States of America

To the families who said yes to adoption
and whose stories inspired these words.

Contents

Foreword

A doption has always been a desire of my heart. Years ago, I'd say to people, "If you have an empty bedroom or an extra bed, you need to adopt!" It's still my belief that every child deserves a home and a family. It's supposed to be that way! What I didn't know then is that every adoption is unique. Where children are from, how old they are when adopted, their life history, and the state of the family adopting them all play a part in an adoptive family's journey.

When Karen first talked with me about writing this book, I was fascinated by her mission: to find out what adoption was *really* like from parents who had traveled the road for several years. Part of Karen's work in Ukraine involved hosting parents who were adopting, so she was well seasoned in that part of the process. I'd seen her at work as a project manager for Orphan's Promise and knew she also clearly understood the plight of children in institutions. Now she was on a quest to get a clear picture of what it was like for adoptive parents and adopted children to become family, and I looked forward to seeing what she would discover.

Our family's adoption journey began years ago. My husband and I had been married for five years. We had a biological son and a biological daughter. It had been my dream to adopt from Korea—a country I'd visited and enjoyed. We began our adoption process when our daughter turned one and our son was three. A year later, our Korean son arrived. We had been matched when he was two weeks old and he was four months old when he finally came.

A couple of years later, a young birth mother was looking for a family for her yet-to-be-born biracial son. To our delight, she chose us. We were over the moon! While our house was loud and lively with four young children, we had no particular issues. I know now that our boys had to deal with thoughtless, rude, and racist comments over the years, but our family stayed close, and adoption was just an accepted part of our story. For years my oldest two children thought all babies came from the airport.

Thirteen years later, when my husband and I were in our fifties, we found ourselves beginning the adoption journey again. We had heard the story of three sisters in Ukraine who were in danger of being split up and adopted separately. I didn't know their names, their ages, or even why they were in the orphanage, but I was deeply troubled by the thought that they might be separated forever.

Less than a year later, we were on our way to Ukraine to add three daughters to our family. They were each two years apart, ages nine, eleven, and thirteen, and our older kids followed the same pattern at ages thirteen, fifteen, seventeen, and nineteen. We learned a bit about the tragedies that had landed the girls in the children's home, and while these details gave us pause, we felt a strong spiritual nudge to proceed. Like so many adoptive families, we assumed love would be enough to heal our new children. We didn't know anyone who had done what we were doing. We had no training or preparation for adopting older children who were wounded by earlier life events. We didn't even know of any books we should read. We were enthusiastically ignorant.

Eighteen years later, I'm much more thoughtful in my perspective. I'm not less enthusiastic about adoption *at all*. But as I've read the stories that Karen chronicles in this book, I've wondered if our family could have been better prepared to navigate the choppy waters of adopting older children with difficult pasts. Like the families Karen interviewed, our journey was fraught with many crises and challenges. Being on the other side of most of it now, I wish I'd known more so I could have met the challenges with more wisdom and grace.

None of us is guaranteed a harmonious family, regardless of whether our children are biological or adopted. There are no easy solutions to growing up or growing together. The most important thing I've learned is that it's my job to love my children and pray for them, and it's God's job to redeem them. Our family is still a work in progress as we continue to accept each other where we are and allow God to keep refining us.

If you're considering embarking on the adventure of adopting, or if you're struggling with some of the harder moments, I know the wisdom found in this book will be both encouraging and challenging. Through the interviews Karen conducted you will enter into the rearview mirror of adoption and perhaps find a piece of your story here. You will certainly have an opportunity to be unified in your decision to adopt as parents and as a family. There is a great opportunity for discussion and prayer. Each of these stories contain a nugget of wisdom. Don't be afraid, but be prepared. We are not called to live comfortably. We are called to make a difference.

Terry Meeuwsen
Cohost, *The 700 Club*
Founder, Orphan's Promise

Author's Note

Due to the sensitivity of the information shared and my desire to protect the identities of children and families, all names of people quoted throughout this book, as well as some identifying details have been changed.

1

Beyond the Yellow Brick Road

My Journey as an Adoption Advocate

Sometimes life takes us places we never expected to go. And in those places God writes a story we never thought would be ours.

—RENEE SWOPE

I t all began with a visit to an orphanage, a world away from my middle-class American life.

I'd arrived in Kyiv, Ukraine, six weeks earlier for what was intended to be an eight-month postcollege adventure. I'd come to serve with my relatives, who at the time had already been living in Ukraine for fourteen years. They were leading the ministry of the Christian Broadcasting Network (CBN)—an organization with a mission to bring the Gospel to the former Soviet Union through the use of mass media and by providing humanitarian assistance. Without much understanding of what serving at the CBN

Kyiv office would mean, I did what many eager yet uncertain college graduates do—I said yes to an adventure.

In the fall of 2004 I was twenty-three years old, fresh out of college, and ready to hit the ground running when I arrived in a country I knew little about. I made my best attempt to jump into Ukrainian life, but the first several months of living in an eastern European country were challenging. I keenly remember the loneliness and floundering feelings I experienced as I adjusted to this new life so far from home. I wondered if I had anything to offer the people I was encountering. My role in the ministry was yet to be defined, and I was unsure of what this year abroad would look like.

Less than two months into my stay, I received the opportunity to participate in a humanitarian aid distribution at an orphanage our office had been working with for several years. I jumped at the chance, as it seemed like the perfect way to get involved, meet some cute children, and understand the needs in the nation. I was told I could interview the director of the facility and write a story about how our organization provided assistance to the orphanage. The assignment seemed simple enough, and it would get me out of the big city and give me a chance to see our ministry's work up close.

After a twelve-hour drive on dilapidated roads, it was nearly nightfall when we pulled up in front of an ominous brick structure known as the *Berdyansk Shkola Internat* (Boarding School). Later I would learn that it was a government institution originally built to house children in a boarding school–like fashion during the country's era of communism. Now, decades later, it was filled primarily with children deemed "social orphans"—those who had been removed from their families because of alcoholism, drug addiction, or neglect. The orphanage looming before me was home to nearly three hundred of these children.

As I exited the van with our team, a little girl who appeared to be around twelve years old made her way through the crowd of children, took me by the hand, and proceeded to escort me into the building. I soon learned that her name was Irina. Nothing about her appearance was particularly remarkable, nor was she the cutest of all the children gathered outside in the dim evening light. It would have been easy to pass her by. But when Irina took my hand, suddenly I was forced to look into eyes that said, "See me." And I did. It was a moment I wouldn't be able to get out of my mind.

I spent three days in that orphanage, most of the time on the playground outside or in the corridor where Irina and her friends lived. I spent every evening with this group of twelve-year-old girls, laughing and joking in my very limited Russian. I was struck by their lonely reality—no papa to tuck them in at night, no mama to wake them up in the morning. I knew that these older kids were likely to be overlooked. Who would tell their stories? Who would see that they didn't become just another statistic? I left determined to find a way to help.

When I returned to Kyiv, I oddly discovered a small school picture of Irina—in the trash can in our ministry building, of all places. To this day, I have no idea how the picture got there. I had left the orphanage inspired to do something, but if I needed an extra nudge or sign from the Lord, then this was it. I taped that little picture into the front of my Bible and began to pray for a family for Irina. She and I also began writing letters to one another, which helped me feel connected to her across the miles.

Perhaps I was drawn to Irina because I realized that, if you stripped away everything I was privileged to have known of safety and love at age twelve, I could have been just like her. Perhaps when I looked into her eyes, I saw myself and an alternate outcome that family and good fortune had spared me. Whatever it was, God used that moment. When Irina placed her sweaty little hand in mine, the course of my life changed in ways I never could have foreseen.

As planned, I wrote an article about my time with the children and the needs of older orphans. It was an impassioned piece that described the charitable work CBN was doing in Ukraine and strongly advocated for the adoption of older children, like the girls I had met. I submitted it to CBN's US office, and to my surprise, they published it on their website. My email address was linked to the article, and within days I was getting inquiries from families in the United States who were curious about exploring the possibility of adopting older children from Ukraine.

Coaching Adoptive Families

Over the next eight months, I became acutely aware of the tragic statistics of crime, prostitution, and suicide surrounding emancipated orphans in the post-Soviet world and was quite cognizant that these older kids were far less likely to be adopted. Deep in my heart, I understood that children belong in families and not in institutions, so I looked up all the verses in the Bible about God defending the orphan and began to use them whenever I could to persuade potential adoptive parents. I knew that children needed families, and I knew that there were families who could parent children. To me, the answer seemed simple: place children in forever homes and end orphanhood in Ukraine.

I gave myself a crash course in international adoption procedures, and before I knew it, I was coaching a handful of families through the process of gathering paperwork and preparing to travel to Ukraine to complete adoptions of older children. I remember emailing families and thinking to myself, "They have no idea that they're communicating with a twenty-three-year-old woman who knows next to nothing about this." Clearly, I was in over my head. At the same time, this new responsibility was exciting, and I was ecstatic when kids exited the orphanage and entered families.

As my initial commitment to CBN's ministry in Ukraine was drawing to a close, I couldn't believe how much had transpired during my short time in the country and how many exciting projects were now in their infancy. A small team in our Kyiv office had just formed to develop a life skills curriculum for volunteers to use with teens exiting orphanages. I had helped produce a documentary promoting adoption, which we were sharing in churches, and I continued to correspond with new families interested in beginning the adoption process. I couldn't imagine walking away from this work or missing out on what God was doing in this land I'd quickly grown to love, but the date on my return ticket to Seattle was fast approaching.

I returned home as planned, but my first goal upon arrival was to enroll in intensive Russian language classes. I was set on returning to Ukraine—only this time, more prepared to speak with those I hoped to help. Within seven months, I was back in Kyiv, picking up where I'd left off.

Over the next few years I would see many of the girls from the first orphanage I visited adopted into loving Christian homes in the US, including little Irina, who captured my heart and changed the course of my life.

While assisting Americans in the adoption process, I also began working with a team of Ukrainians in our Kyiv office on a national adoption campaign aimed at Ukrainian families and the Ukrainian church. At that time, adoption was a relatively new concept in Ukraine, as it had previously been shrouded in shame and secrecy. But as we began to share about several Ukrainian families who had been called to adopt, we started to see God birth an adoption movement in the country.

Knowing that not all children could or would be adopted, our team continued to develop and refine a curriculum that could be used in orphanages to prepare kids spiritually, physically, socially, emotionally, and mentally for life outside the orphanage. Each summer we'd put on camps in government orphanages, which enabled us to develop relationships with kids, share our faith, and teach lessons and life skills from our curriculum. Through these various projects, I found my purpose and passion: caring for orphans and calling families to consider adoption. Over time, I would see hundreds of orphans welcomed into families, both in Ukraine and in America.

Hospitality House Kyiv

Four years after my first orphanage visit, I was still ministering in Ukraine with no plans to leave. By this time, my volunteer position had turned into an official job with Orphan's Promise, which at that time was a new ministry of CBN that had been established specifically to care for the needs of orphans in Ukraine. Over the next ten years, Orphan's Promise would expand its work to reach children in over sixty nations around the globe, with the mission of bringing orphaned and vulnerable children from "at risk" to thriving.

As my local team's work kept growing, we began bringing groups of orphans to the United States each Christmas to perform a heartwarming children's musical that helped raise awareness about the needs of orphans in Ukraine. As a result of these kids traveling to the US and staying with host families, I saw dozens more children adopted.

Seeing the success of such trips, I was led to begin a separate hosting program with a friend of mine in the US. Together, we brought a group of Ukrainian children to our home church in Washington for a month each summer, where they had an opportunity to be hosted by families, get a break from orphanage life, and experience American culture. I was all about advocacy, advocacy, advocacy!

Because of my work with Orphan's Promise and my own personal interest in advocating for children, I was continually introduced to Americans who were traveling to Ukraine to adopt. I'd get an email about a family stuck in Kyiv for some reason, meet them for a meal, try to ease their worries about the adoption process, and be a friendly, English-speaking face to counteract the culture shock they were experiencing. These interactions were a source of joy, as I felt I could provide encouragement and help families gain realistic expectations concerning the adoption timeline and navigating Ukrainian bureaucracy.

One summer, I ran into a lovely couple from Texas who happened to be stuck longer than normal waiting for a second appointment at the state department for adoption. They were hoping I could provide advice or guide them toward adoptable kids in the age range they were looking for. After hanging out with this family a couple of times, I did what anyone would do for perfect strangers—I invited them to move in with me. And they did what anyone would do when a perfect stranger offers such a proposal—they accepted!

We spent numerous late nights around the dinner table, talking about adoption, missions, books, relationships, the Bible, and following Jesus. The Lord used the time with this family to reveal to me how much I enjoy opening my home and life to adoptive families. Because of this experience, I began to pray about starting a formal hospitality ministry for adoptive families in Ukraine and started to explore what that might look like. God answered my prayer only six months later in the form of an apartment that made the ministry possible. With the financial support of Orphan's Promise and my church in Kyiv, I was able to move into this larger space that was near to both the city center and the adoption department. Thus, "Hospitality House Kyiv" was born.

Within days of moving into my apartment in February of 2011, I already had guests. I launched a new blog to express my desire to give adoptive families a free and comfortable place to stay while in the city, and I immediately received numerous email inquiries. Some people were surprised that I'd be willing to open my home to strangers, but I determined that if the US government had done background checks on these families and approved them to adopt children, the chances were good that I wouldn't be hosting any serial killers.

Over the ensuing weeks and months, I was overwhelmed by the response from families who were either bright-eyed and bushy-tailed at the beginning of their adoption journey or worn out and weary after six-plus weeks in a foreign country and just trying to keep it together long enough to cross the finish line. My day planner was chock full of families arriving and departing, and my washing machine was working overtime. Since I didn't have a dryer, I came up with creative ways to string clothes lines around my apartment to ensure quick drying times.

As families entered my home, I reveled in listening to like-minded people share stories of what led them to adopt and the miraculous ways funding arrived in time. By the end of the first year of opening my home, I had hosted thirty-four families, and I entered into the second year with even more enthusiasm. More couples in my home meant more children were gaining families.

Caution Ahead

I continued to celebrate my "happy-ending," Cinderella-like adoption stories by writing about them in my blog, *Beauty from the Ashes*. I capitalized on stories of redemption, and I loved crafting one-page renditions of how a family embraced a child and transformed a life. They were indeed beautiful stories, and I truly believed what I was writing. The problem was that many of the stories were short-sighted or incomplete. They implied that if we could just get children out of awful orphanages, all would be well. However, I was learning that it wasn't that simple. While trumpeting the beauty of adoption on the one hand, another part of me was becoming more cautious, wondering how I could provide better support for adoptive families and more education for those who were considering adopting older children.

I kept in touch with many families in the US who had adopted Ukrainian children, and I began hearing these parents describe the effects of early childhood trauma on their children's ability to attach, develop healthy relationships, and regulate their behaviors and emotions. Some families who had successfully parented biological children and entered into adoption with a "more love to give" attitude were drowning in tumultuous seas and grasping for a lifeline.

Sometimes I found myself in a quandary when the families I was hosting, still in the beginning stages of their adoption process, would sit on my couch and tell stories of how they'd hosted their child and fallen in love with him or her. Inevitably, they would ask my opinion about something related to adoption or ask me how other families were doing who were already back in the States with their kids. Of course, these families were looking for reassurance, wanting to hear happy or encouraging stories.

I struggled with the tension surrounding how much to share about the harder side of adoption for fear that it would scare people away. To what degree would telling them real and difficult stories help or hurt? After all, I mused, they'd come this far, and they probably wouldn't be able to digest the hard things until they had tough times themselves. What purpose would it serve to worry them or perhaps cause them to question their decision? So, usually, I didn't say much at all, for fear of saying the wrong thing. I still think that was the right choice. Putting myself in their shoes, I wouldn't have wanted to hear hard stories at that stage in the game.

As I grappled with these tensions, I had the opportunity to attend a reunion for families who had adopted older Ukrainian children a couple of years before. Thirteen adopted kids were present, along with their families. All of these kids, now in their teens, had been adopted as a result of the hosting trips I'd helped organize.

As we gathered the kids for a group photo, they stood beaming with arms around one another. It was the perfect Facebook moment, with all those bright and happy faces guaranteed to score hundreds of "likes." As the picture was being snapped, I leaned over to my friend (mama to four adopted kids, all who have experienced their share of complex trauma) and said, "Wow, look at all these lives we've changed!" Then, nodding toward the parents, I added jokingly, "And look how many lives we may have ruined."

We both chuckled in a dark comedic way that only people in the adoption community who have dealt with trauma can fully understand. My comment was in jest, and we both knew it. However, as the words left my lips, I couldn't minimize the fact that the lives of these families had been drastically altered by saying yes to adoption, and that I had encouraged them to do so. While blogs and Facebook are perfect platforms for celebrating adoption, many adoptive families quickly realize that social media is not the best outlet for sharing their daily trials. As a result, relatives and friends who watched a very public journey to "bring a child home" no longer knew how these families were really doing and what challenges they faced.

As is true with many things in life, hindsight is often twenty-twenty. Sometimes it's only in looking through the rearview mirror that we can see things with a new perspective. I was increasingly realizing that I needed to have a more thoughtful and educated approach to advocacy—and perhaps the church in North America needed this as well. The church was waking up to the needs of the orphaned and vulnerable around the world and calling people to respond. But were those answering the call being given *all* the information? Were they adequately equipped for what was to come?

I began to consider how I could go about listening more deeply to the stories of adoptive families. How could I honor their voices? And, perhaps just as important, how could I gather firsthand knowledge of realities that might help prepare prospective adoptive families to ride the ups and downs of the journey?

Road Trip!

Someone once told me that, considering all the families I have met and worked with, I've probably collected enough stories to write a book! Yet I have not done so lightly. I recognize that anytime a delicate subject such as adoption comes up, there are myriad views, and those views are largely based on personal experiences. By no means do I pretend to be an expert on adoption. I've never adopted a child, nor do I have a degree in child psychology or counseling. Many times I questioned if I was even *qualified* to write a book about adoption. But in these moments of doubt, I was assured by the adoptive families I encountered that I have an important story to tell from a unique vantage point. Having witnessed the adoption journey of well over two hundred families, I've been provided a wide-angle lens with which to see trends and patterns that others may not have noticed or considered.

Over the fourteen years I've worked within the realm of orphan care and advocacy, I have been on my own personal journey of making sense of the complex world of adoption. I have traveled the road from passionate advocate to skeptical critic and back again, sometimes landing on both perspectives in the same day. On many days I have been tempted to succumb to disillusionment. I've struggled with the knowledge that faithful adoptive families show up at church every Sunday looking like they have it all together, when in truth there's deep hurt and confusion at home. And I've asked myself again and again what I can possibly do to help.

To begin to answer this question, I knew I needed to return to the source: the families I hosted in my home in Ukraine. After much prayer and seeking counsel, I decided to take several months away from my life and work in Ukraine and spend time with "my" families in the US, hearing their hearts and discovering more of what they've experienced and learned since adopting.

Shortly after moving into my apartment in Kyiv that would become the Hospitality House, I mounted a large map in the entryway, where I pinned the location of every adoptive family who had ever stayed with me. After gazing at the hundreds of names on my map and seeing those names span across the US, I decided that a road trip would be the best way to connect with these families and document their post-adoption stories. I sent out a test email to a group of families to see if any of them would be open to being interviewed and was soon overwhelmed at the positive responses that filled my inbox.

So I set out on an ambitious venture: I would plot a four-month road trip across the country to visit and learn from the many families who had stayed with me. I'd ask the parents questions like: Had they been prepared for their adoption journey? What would they have done differently? How were their adopted children finding healing? How were their biological children affected? What were the most important lessons they learned? How would they counsel prospective adoptive families? And—perhaps the deepest question of all—where was God in all of this?

My journey would take me from Washington state to Maine, from Georgia to Hawaii and many places in between. I would cover 14,200 road miles (not counting the flight to Hawaii!) and 38 states. Surely, it would be the trip of a lifetime! I wasn't sure I was ready, but I was willing. Four months later, I was on my way, eager to listen to the real experts and document everything I learned.

2

Are We Going in the Right Direction?

Answering the Call to Adopt

Can adoption be an incredible thing? Yes. But it's dangerous to make it too slick on the outside and to market adoption as something that's for everyone, making people feel that if they're not doing it, they're not good Christians.

—ADOPTIVE FATHER

After living outside my home country for over a decade, my trip was an extraordinary opportunity to explore parts of the United States that I'd never seen before. I was fortunate to have several friends and family members meet up with me along the way and become co-pilots on some of the longer driving days. I've joked that after completing this trip I could not only write a book about adoption but also one on road-tripping across America: best food stops, worst coffee, most interesting landmarks, good audio books and other productive and creative ways to pass time in the car, and even what makes some bed sheets more comfortable than others.

As I prepared to visit adoptive families across the US, I looked forward to hearing about what had motivated them to pursue adoption and what they had experienced so far on their journey. But every few days, when my GPS brought me to a new driveway, I was reminded that my journey needed to be approached with the utmost care. I'd stroll up to an adoptive family's front door, duffle bag in hand, take a deep breath, and knock. I'd not seen some of these families in years, and here I was coming into their homes and asking them to share the most vulnerable parts of their adoption experience so I could have a bird's-eye view of the inner workings of their family. It amazed me how easy it was to reconnect with these people. United by shared experiences in Ukraine, we seamlessly picked up where we had left off.

The 63 families I interviewed had adopted a combined total of 141 Ukrainian children. The vast majority of the families had adopted older children; the average age of a child at the time of adoption was eleven. Though I primarily interviewed the parents, I also had opportunities to interview a handful of adopted teens and some of the biological children. As I spent time with these families and conducted formal interviews, they shared very personal and intimate details of their adoption journey in hopes that their stories would help educate and encourage, and offer empathy to families in similar situations. I am forever grateful for their vulnerability and trust in me.

I discovered that these families had decided to adopt from Ukraine for several reasons. Some had gotten to know their future children through a hosting program. Some had been stirred by listings online of children with illnesses or special needs, which meant that a Ukrainian family would be far less likely to adopt them, due to the overall lack of resources for these children in Ukraine. Others had heard the same horror stories that first gripped me about teens aging out of orphanages and turning to crime and prostitution to survive. Many parents were motivated to rescue a child from the dismal outcome of human trafficking. All of them wanted to provide children in need with a family, a future, and a better life.

Three books were referenced over and over in the course of my interviews. If you keep up with popular Christian nonfiction, you are likely to be familiar with at least one of these titles: *Crazy Love* by Francis Chan, *The Hole in Our Gospel* by Richard Stearns, and *Radical* by David Platt. Published between 2008 and 2010, these books rose quickly on the best-seller lists, their messages permeating the thinking of many evangelical Christian communities in North America. The books are not about adoption, but they confront the Western status quo, challenging readers to examine how they are living out their Christianity in practical ways.

Many families shared that one or more of these books had challenged them to put their faith into action and consider stepping out of their comfort zones into the realm of adoption. Twenty-three percent said that they'd heard a message or sermon encouraging adoption that directly affected their decision to adopt, and 90 percent stated that they felt called by God to adopt. In decades past, the motivation to adopt was usually the inability to become pregnant, but only 13 percent of those I interviewed had no biological children and had wanted to build their family through adoption. Today it is clear that in Christian circles, more people are motivated to adopt by a higher calling to demonstrate their faith in visible ways.

In *Radical*, David Platt writes, "You and I can choose to continue with business as usual in the Christian life and in the church as a whole, enjoying success based on the standards defined by the culture around us. Or we can take an honest look at the Jesus of the Bible and dare to ask what the consequences might be if we really believed him and really obeyed him."[1] The result: thousands of Christians have become passionate about living out their faith radically. To the readers I interviewed, this meant adopting children who needed families.

Marketing Adoption

I consider the voices of those like Francis Chan and David Platt to be akin to the voices of prophets. They have witnessed an American church that is largely asleep and more inwardly than outwardly focused. In response they, like the great prophets of the Bible, have held up a mirror that reflects what is wrong, and they've issued a battle cry to make it right. The messages of these books call Christ-

36

followers to live out the teachings of Jesus in a tangible way.

There is no doubt that we need such prophetic voices. As I read the words of Francis Chan in *Crazy Love,* I was challenged to examine my heart and consider the ways I live out *American* Christianity instead of *biblical* Christianity. The church desperately needs teachers who can point us back to true north when the world skews our views and desires. However, we equally need the voices and giftings of teachers who can *inform* and *equip* us for the work at hand.

One area where we need more accurate information concerns how many children in the world are even available for adoption. There is a lot of misinformation and misrepresentation regarding statistics that portray the needs of orphans and unparented children. I believe this misrepresentation has fueled much of the church's response. In a world inundated with information, it's easy to inadvertently misuse statistics when encouraging families to adopt.

United Nations Children's Fund (UNICEF), the agency often cited for its statistics of orphans and vulnerable children, notes there are 140 million orphans worldwide. When people hear that number, they often assume it means there are 140 million children in need of families, but that is not the case. The number provided by UNICEF represents children throughout the world who have lost one or both parents. It is estimated that, of the 140 million children, 15.1 million are classified as *double* orphans (children who have lost both parents).[2] Global estimates point to somewhere between 2 million[3] to 8 million[4] children living in orphanages or children's homes around the world,[*] and data shows that 80 percent of children in institutions have living relatives or parents.[5] As these numbers indicate, not all children classified as orphans, or even those living in institutions, are available for adoption.

I saw this illustrated firsthand as I began working with children in government orphanages in Ukraine. As I spoke to children I met, I learned very quickly that few were orphaned due to the loss of a parent. More often, the government had terminated the parents' rights or had removed the children from their homes as a result of abuse, neglect, or a parent's substance addiction. The majority of children I met were not legally free to be adopted. According to a 2019 report in Ukraine, there are an estimated 106,000 children living in 751 orphanages throughout the country. Of those, 92 percent have at least one living parent, while only 8 percent are true orphans. And of the 106,000 living in institutions, only about 6,000 are available for adoption.[6]

Sadly, institutions in Ukraine and elsewhere in the world are full of children who are stuck in a system because of their legal status. Until recently, concrete efforts to restore them to biological family members or find local foster or adoption solutions were quite rare; now programs are moving in that direction.

---

[*] These numbers are likely low due to lack of data from many countries and the large number of unregistered institutions.

Among the families I interviewed, 70 percent of the adopted children had a living parent at the time of their adoption. Only 20 percent had parents who were confirmed or believed to be deceased. For the rest of the children, the status of their parents was unknown at the time of the adoption; in many of these cases the children had been institutionalized since birth.

Children who are removed from a home at an older age have very different needs than those whose parents have died. As we promote adoption, we must be clear about the kind of preparation families need to parent children who come from difficult backgrounds.* As I traveled from coast to coast and listened to adoptive families' differing and often challenging stories, I continued to ask myself: Where have we gotten the messaging wrong, perhaps withheld

---

* The wisdom of experts in trauma-informed care and attachment disorders, for example, is a great place to start. *Trauma-informed care* is a concept that has been evolving over the last thirty years, as professionals have gained a greater understanding of post-traumatic stress disorder through studying the post effects of war. The understanding of trauma then extended to work with children and the development of evidence-based models of trauma treatment to facilitate resilience and recovery. *Attachment disorders* are psychiatrically diagnosed disorders that are common in children who experienced abuse and neglect in early years. They are characterized by problems in emotionally attaching to others, specifically parents or caregivers. See "Attachment Disorders," American Academy of Child and Adolescent Psychiatry, January 2014, https://www.aacap.org/AACAP/Families_ and_Youth/ Facts_for_Families/FFF-Guide/Attachment-Disorders-085.aspx.

information, or misrepresented the global need for adoption? How can we present the messaging around adoption in a more transparent and helpful way?

What I've discovered is that a prophetic voice not coupled with a teaching or pastoring voice is about as effective as a blitz evangelism mission in which there's no follow-up to ensure that individuals are supported in following Jesus in their daily lives. Yes, we need to advocate and invite believers to respond to the needs of children, but we need to do so with honesty and transparency about what following the call will likely entail. A worthy cause might rally the troops, but glamorizing it won't provide the strength or wisdom needed to weather the storms that are likely to follow.

Mixed Messages

The families I interviewed who'd been inspired to adopt by such prophetic voices as those mentioned earlier, said their decision was largely met with support and affirmation. Though some admitted that they'd heard their fair share of negative adoption stories (typically told by parents, relatives, or concerned friends trying to dissuade them), most felt that the messages being painted by the evangelical church and the adoption community at large were overwhelmingly positive.

This was certainly true for David and his wife, Sharon, who adopted two Ukrainian girls in the span of one year. "There is almost no literature on the difficult stories," David said. "Until you look at attachment disorder 'disaster blogs,' you don't really see it. The primary message coming from inside the church is about the nobility of adopting." Another adoptive father commented, "Perhaps we heard only what we wanted to hear, but truly it seems like we didn't hear many negative stories." Conversely, the voices of the few naysayers, who had often heard horror stories, were so extreme that some families felt their only option was to cover their ears and keep moving forward, confident that God was calling them to adopt.

The Bower family adopted an eight-year-old boy from Ukraine. The parents shared that it was hard to balance the positive and negative messages they were receiving as they made the decision to adopt. "I didn't need naysayers," said Cara, the mother. "What I needed were *truth-tellers*. People who would say, 'Yes, it sucks at times.' I think the church and some organizations have romanticized this to a degree. You can't just go get your princess and make her have curly hair and love pink and think about how you are going to paint her nails. It's just not like that. If you're looking for your own recognition and attention, you shouldn't adopt. We need to be asking, 'What's your motive? Are you both in this together? What research have you done?' You need to become quite informed."

Several families noted that other adoptive families or those in the adoption community remained positive advocates while the family was going through the paperwork process, but afterward these same advocates initiated the family into a new "club." Families suddenly found themselves being added to social media discussion groups they'd previously been unaware of. No one was added to the "PTSD Trauma Adoption Group" until *after* they came home with their child.

One of the adoptive mothers I interviewed commented, "I wish there was more transparency. There was an adoptive mom here in our town who had teens, three of whom were adopted. When I was preparing my paperwork she'd [sweetly] ask, 'How's it going?' Shortly after we got home, she pulled me aside and asked very candidly in a whisper, 'So how are you *really* doing?' She seemed to know that a nightmare was coming—but hadn't wanted to say anything before the adoption was complete."

Another mother, who walked through a devastating experience that resulted in her two adopted children being moved to other homes, told me that her family felt deceived by a Christian hosting organization. This group had done a hard sell on adoption and led the family to believe that the challenging situations they'd heard of were only outliers who spoke loudly. The mother also felt that her negative experiences were suppressed by other adoptive families who didn't want adoption framed in a damaging light. When disturbing information about their adopted child's sexual behavior came to light, those who had once been their advocates suddenly withdrew their support. "For these people," she said, "adoption has become an idol—and you don't want to taint the reputation of your idol. So it's 'see no evil, hear no evil' because they're trying to promote it and trying to recruit people and, in some cases, even trying to look like heroes. For us, in the end, when things went really, *really* wrong, all the people who'd escorted us in and told us it was going to be great didn't want to hear about our experience."

One couple I interviewed, Nick and Sarah Tayler, candidly admitted that they got caught up in the spirit of being activated without being fully prepared for the adoption they chose. Today, they feel strongly that the church and other Christian entities have marketed adoption without full disclosure surrounding the spectrum of challenges. Nick shared:

> I continue to hear the same thing. Whether it's [written on] a social service billboard in the city about adoption or [shared] through the church or the best Christian organizations, it's all the same message: "If you just adopt, this will be the best thing for your family and the best thing for these waiting kids." And I don't think that's true. Yes, for the right families, with eyes wide open, it can be because God does work like this and He can use adoption to pull people in and redeem a bad situation. But you need to have everything on the table about how it could go. In the megachurch evangelical culture, we get off track when anything is overly marketed. If there was more transparency, probably not as many people would adopt, but those who did would be so much more successful because they'd be prepared.

I have reflected on the implications of this conversation many times. I've been guilty of marketing adoption by sharing the beauty and neglecting to share the pain. We tend to package things in the most attractive way possible. We've done it with our faith, and we've done it with adoption. As humans, we gravitate toward happy, redemptive stories. I believe God created us this way. It's why we get depressed when we watch the evening news. It's also why the networks add some happy stories at the end, about things like a pet being rescued, in order to conclude on a high note and not leave us feeling as if the world is in total chaos. We resonate with stories of redemption because it's what we long for in all areas of our lives. Yes, there is a war in Syria, and yes, there is an opioid epidemic in the United States, but that fireman rescued a little girl and her kitten from a burning building, so at least we can go to bed with a glimmer of hope.

Redemption is our hope of heaven; praise God that He allows us to glimpse scenes of that redemption here on earth. The danger is when we inoculate ourselves from the whole truth by listening only to stories with positive narratives. When we hear stories framed in only one light, we end up surprised when *our* narrative doesn't turn out quite as bright. And we may walk away feeling misled by the stories we were told, as if we were given the short end of the stick.

Overspiritualizing Adoption

I love how Scripture directly correlates the physical and spiritual aspects of adoption. The beauty of children being adopted into loving families is naturally associated with God adopting us through His Son, Jesus Christ. This was actually one of the first truths that captivated my heart as I felt led to advocate for the orphan. I loved thinking about how adoption parallels our faith journey and our inclusion into God's family. I have shared this message in churches and conferences and have been encouraged by Romans 8:15–17 (emphasis mine): "The Spirit you received does not make you slaves, so that you live in fear again; rather, the Spirit you received brought about your *adoption* to sonship. And by him we cry, 'Abba, Father.' The Spirit himself testifies with our spirit that we are God's children. Now if we are children, then we are heirs—*heirs of God* and co-heirs with Christ, if indeed we share in his sufferings in order that we may also share in his glory."

Many of the families I interviewed also said that this message was a motivating factor in their adoption story. However, I think we need to be cautious about using language that leads people to believe: "I was adopted by God; therefore, I must adopt." We may use the spiritual aspects of adoption to motivate families to consider adopting, but we cannot avoid the fact that the same Gospel that reflects adoption is also one that reflects suffering.

We are very good at selling the message of social justice by showcasing inspiring stories of redemption. These are the stories that go viral on social media. We tell stories that have happy endings because they inspire people to action and because they fill us with hope. But we do a disservice to families and children when we overspiritualize adoption and leave off the hard truths about what such a decision will require.

A good friend of mine, Jason, is an adoptive dad and pastor who has shared some of his concerns about how the dialogue surrounding adoption often equates adoption to the Gospel. He has written about this topic on his blog, saying:

> The parallels between the Gospel and adoption are beautiful, but some take this too far. Though adoption allows us to physically see certain spiritual realities of the Gospel of Jesus, adoption is not the Gospel. It can definitely be a fruit of the Gospel, but for the Church, the opportunity to care for orphans is a discipleship issue. It shouldn't be a cause. It shouldn't be a campaign. . . . It's a calling. It's a good calling, but it's not a calling for everyone. We have to be careful that we don't elevate the call to adopt to being more significant [than] other calls that are also fruit of the Gospel.[7]

Though not all families are called to adopt, there is no doubt that as followers of Christ, we are called to respond to the needs of the vulnerable. We cannot overlook the orphan, widow, refugee, or the poor. Scripture makes it clear that these people groups are beloved by our Father, and as we seek His heart we should be convicted and led to care for, love, and befriend those He names throughout Scripture. But being led to the act of adopting is a unique call, and we must do all we can to equip those who are called—not use guilt or Christian trends to pressure unprepared families. One of my friends who is an adoptive mother recently shared with me, "I always try to scare people out of adoption with my crazy stories. I figure if they're truly called to adopt, then what I share with them won't stop them from answering God's call."

There are a variety of ways to respond to the global need to provide permanence for children. That may mean adoption for some families, or it may mean supporting other efforts like strengthening families in crisis or building up the capacity of developing nations to reach their orphans and at-risk children. Bottom line, churches and organizations are wise to use a multifaceted approach as they promote caring for the vulnerable rather than portraying a message that adopting is the only "Christian" thing to do.

Counting the Cost

I have yet to hear a sermon, attend a conference, or see a promotional video about an adoption story in crisis, where biological children become reclusive or resentful or adoptive families suffer the effects of secondary trauma and PTSD. I have a feeling that people wouldn't be rushing to sign up to adopt a child after hearing such a message. But for those who are indeed *called* to adopt, the Gospel of Luke offers a perspective that must be kept in mind.

In a discussion with His disciples, Jesus said, "Suppose one of you wants to build a tower. Won't you first sit down and estimate the cost to see if you have enough money to complete it? For if you lay the foundation and are not able to finish it, everyone who sees it will ridicule you, saying, 'This person began to build and wasn't able to finish' " (Luke 14:28–30). Jesus was talking about what it means to live a life of obedience to Him and how important it is to count the cost before signing up to be His follower.

In my research, I found that nearly all the families who felt called and motivated to adopt *did* count the cost of adoption in terms of the financial commitment involved and the sacrifices they'd have to make in their standard of living when adding another child to their family. For many families, finances were practically their entire focus in the beginning, as the money needed to complete an adoption seemed to be the biggest hurdle to overcome. They reasoned that if God provided the funding then He would make a way in all other areas of the adoption.

While I don't discount the goodness of God in providing the finances needed to complete an adoption, I think that some families focus too intently on the financial aspects and don't pause long enough to count the emotional, physical, and spiritual costs. As one mother reflected, "I was a billion percent naive. We got so wrapped up in the preparation for the house and all the romanticized notions of bringing home a child. I look back now and see we were blissfully ignorant."

Even the most prepared and well-read families I interviewed, however, conceded that they began their adoption journey with some degree of rose tint in their glasses. They simply did not know what they did not know. As they glance in the rearview mirror now, many wish they could go back and remove their rose-colored glasses so they'd have had a clearer view of the road ahead.

For Reflection or Group Discussion

1. In what ways have you heard messaging from the church encourage or discourage adoption?

2. Do you feel that you hear balanced perspectives of positives and negatives in adoption stories?

3. Did seeing adoption mirrored in the Gospel inspire you or anyone you know in the adoption journey? If so, how?

4. Did you or anyone you know who has adopted count the cost emotionally, spiritually, socially, as well as financially before starting the process?

not so much

The Collision of Expectations and Reality

Removing the Rose-Colored Glasses

I thought if God was in the adoption, it was going to be good.
I had the misunderstanding that "good" meant smooth.

—ADOPTIVE MOTHER

I magine that you're engaged and about to be married. You're in the butterflies-in-your-stomach stage, and when your loved one walks in, your heart swells with joy and excitement. All you can focus on are the wedding plans—flowers, cake, gift registries—envisioning how you'll set up the perfect home with your spouse. You picture how that luxurious bedding will look in your ideally decorated room and how you're going to host friends and family around your new dining room table. Your eyes are on that glorious wedding day, and you glow with premarital bliss.

Now, with this idyllic picture in your mind, imagine that you mistakenly find yourself walking into a marriage seminar filled with couples who are attending counseling for infidelity, addiction, and years of unresolved anger and resentment. These are marriages on the verge of divorce, and there are no smiling faces in the room. Instead, you see tears and tissues. Before you can fully digest the scene, a woman walks up to you and says, "I wish I'd never gotten married. It has ruined my life."

What would your reaction be? Would you call the whole thing off and walk away? After all, why risk being hurt or looking incompetent or ruining your life and family? Would you cover your eyes and ears, bolt out the door, and declare loudly, "No! This will *never* happen to me and my spouse. We love each other! We would never even dream of being unfaithful. This won't be *our* story." Caught up in current emotions and expectations, unable to entertain the thought of suffering in the future, would you drown out the naysayers and run back to the group of glowing brides and grooms at the wedding expo you originally meant to attend? Would you return to your search for the perfect dress, flowers, cake, moving in a straight line toward the idealistic goal?

There is another response to this same scenario: You could pause, take a deep breath, look at yourself in the mirror, and say, "Wow, there is a lot of risk involved in getting married. Do I really want to get married (adopt!) knowing that it will likely be hard? If the answer is yes, then is there anything I can do now to prevent these hard things from happening? How can I prepare today to handle the inevitable challenges that will come? Where will our family turn for help when hard circumstances threaten to pull us apart?"

Happily Ever After?

It's easy to understand why many of us have a fascination with orphans. After all, they're the heroes of many wildly popular American films. Disney has made millions using orphans in leading roles—from animal characters like Dumbo, Bambi, and Simba, to young orphaned boys like Peter Pan and Aladdin—all searching for a place to belong. We also pay tribute to the orphaned royalty of Cinderella, Snow White, and the recent additions of Anna and Elsa. It's clear that Disney loves orphans, and so do entertainment seekers. We cheer for these orphans because they're underdogs, and we want them to make it. So we soak up their stories, and from afar we love the orphan.

At least we love the orphans we see triumphing on the screen. Nowhere in the Disney films do we see our heroes rage at, lie to, manipulate, curse, hate, or reject the ones who come to "rescue" and "save" them. I think Disney realizes that a more realistic plotline wouldn't appeal to anybody. And yet many of these negative behaviors are a reality of adoption, especially with older children.

The orphaned spirit at its worst definitely isn't entertaining. Adoptive families can experience overwhelming challenges as they attempt to love their children well. Families who lovingly pursue adoption with Disneyland expectations sometimes find themselves far afield from the experience of happily ever after.

Over several months of conversing with parents, I uncovered a wide variety of expectations surrounding raising adopted children. Some families said they went in with no expectations, while others had many. Though a number of families admitted that they were adorned with rose-colored glasses, others shared that they really tried to prepare for the worst so they could be pleasantly surprised if things weren't as bad as some of the books warned (gotta love their optimism).

The majority of families who had done their fair share of preparation through reading and classes felt that they were well versed in things they expected to confront. However, they often dealt with a variety of issues they didn't see coming. Or they hadn't fully grasped what an issue would actually be like until they were dealing with it firsthand. There was one statement I heard repeated in interview after interview, and it went something like this: "We knew that adoption would be hard; we just didn't understand *how hard* it would be or what our hard would be."

Sabrina and her husband, Jack, adopted their daughter when she was ten and shared that it was hard not to romanticize the unknowns of adoption. "It's human nature because none of us would do anything if we didn't glamorize or romanticize things to some degree," Sabrina said. "If we all operated in the mode of, 'Oh, it's going to be horrible, and they are going to be a demon child, and they'll call me names and hate me,' nobody would ever do it. I remember thinking that all they need is love—every child deserves to be loved—that's all they need," she added with a laugh. "Nope—that's super important, and it starts there, but they need a lot more than just love. I thought she'd need us or need me, but I really feel like she won't allow herself to need anyone, and that surprised me. I realize we got a gem of a daughter, and yet it's *still* so hard."

When Love Is Not Enough

My friend and colleague Jayne Schooler, one of the authors of the book *Wounded Children, Healing Homes*, often shares that, in her experience, most couples enter into adoption wearing two signs. The one on their front says Love Is Enough, and the sign on their back says And It Won't Happen to Us. The beliefs, she says, are often unconscious, but they're there nonetheless. When I shared this sentiment with many of the families I interviewed, it clearly struck a chord. "Yes! That was us," they cried. "We truly thought that love would be enough to change our child, or we really wanted to believe it would be enough." It didn't take long after arriving home for reality to set in and these same "love is enough" families realized that their children, who had typically experienced significant childhood trauma, would need a lot more than love to be transformed and healed.

Derek and Lucy had already raised two daughters when they journeyed to Ukraine to bring home two sons in two years. "We thought they'd join the family and we'd love them and they'd be fine," Lucy said. "[But] this was before we knew about or understood childhood trauma. Perhaps God is gracious and only shows you so much. I don't doubt we were called to it. But how I view it has changed. At first, I thought the hard part was the paperwork, and then we got to Ukraine and I thought the hard part was completing the in-country process. Then one night after getting home, as I lay in bed, I said out loud to my husband, 'I think maybe the hard part is just beginning.' "

Kendra Smith and her husband, Dan, were in their early thirties when they adopted sixteen-year-old Andre and his twelve-year-old sister, Nina, from Ukraine. Adopting older children from the other side of the world had never been their plan or something they would have even considered, but hosting these siblings in their home through a summer program for orphans in 2014 set them on a new course.

The Smiths couldn't deny that God had placed Andre and Nina in front of them for a reason, and other families in their community rallied around them and advocated for the siblings' adoption. United with a clear calling from God, big hearts, and hopes that a family would bring healing to Andre and Nina, the Smiths were determined to give their all to provide a safe home for the Ukrainian brother and sister.

Kendra and Dan were far from naive. They knew adopting older kids would be a challenge. Challenge, however, took on new meaning as they completed the adoption in Ukraine and then began to integrate the siblings into their already established family with two young biological daughters.

As I sat in the Smith's cozy living room, nearly four years after they brought home their two adopted children, Dan and Kendra settled in side by side on the couch. They appeared a bit nervous, perhaps wondering what kinds of questions I'd be asking. But as we chatted into the late evening hours, any anxiety vanished; they shared their experiences with vulnerability and a good dose of comic relief.

"When Andre first came to our family, he would run when things got hard," said Dan. "Any correction I gave him would make him super mad and he would leave. Last October was the darkest part of our journey when he left for four days. I remember thinking, 'Oh my gosh, I brought this kid here to be homeless? I feel like a complete failure. What are we going to do?' Looking back, in many ways we thought if we could just get them here, they'd be okay. And in many ways they are . . . but this has been incredibly hard for them and for us."

When they traveled to Ukraine to bring Andre and Nina home, the Smiths didn't foresee a future involving numerous police visits, their younger biological daughters being bullied, search parties for their runaway teens, forced counseling sessions, or the endless days Nina would lock herself in her room and refuse to eat. Their cozy suburban life started to feel like a reality TV show, starring a chaotic and colorful cast of characters including cops, social workers, psychologists, school administrators, relatives, neighbors, and friends. It felt like the whole world was watching, and yet the loneliness of their journey was over-whelming at times. Kendra shared that there were many days when she questioned if adoption had been the right decision for any of them.

> Three months in, we thought, "What have we done?" Honestly, sometimes I still think that way. My goal on some days is simply not to go crazy. I mean, we see the cops at our house and think, "What are we doing?" Our extended family members were naysayers to begin with, so it was hard to get the I-told-you-so vibes when things got crazy.

> One day I asked my (adopted) son what he thought about adoption and asked him what is best for kids—to be adopted or to stay where they were. He said, "It's better to be adopted for the kid—but probably bad for the family." I was shocked that he said that. I think he sees how stressful it is—especially the challenges we've had with his sister. There are moments when I think, "Our lives would be so different if we hadn't done this." But I also don't think it's a common American thing to accept struggle.

Dan interjected, "Maybe as Americans we think their lives will be so much better here and we can fix them, but I don't know if I've changed the trajectory of their lives simply by bringing them to America. All the same possi-bilities still exist, but I do know God has put them in our lives to love and care for them. It's exhausting, but I don't think as Christians we're called to live a life that is easy or stress-free."

Our two-and-a-half-hour conversation would have left a casual observer deeply confused. One moment Kendra was recounting midnight moments of having to call the police to report their missing child and the heartache of suspecting that her teen daughter was experimenting with drugs, and the next moment she quite literally stated, "I'm living the dream," as she shared about the growth and maturity they've seen in their adopted son in recent months. Our conversation contained good long belly laughs, but we passed the tissue box more than once. Like many adoptive families, the Smith's story is full of paradox.

"Yes, it's really, really hard," Kendra said. "But I've learned so much about loving when it's hard. It's so difficult to love and then be slapped in the face by the person you are trying to love. But that's what Jesus shows us to do. I'd tell someone, 'If you feel called to adopt, I'll be there for you.'" She paused, smiled, laughed a little, and added, "But, I'll also tell you it isn't all rainbows and unicorns and it can really suck sometimes."

Facing Rejection

Many families I spoke with were unprepared for how early childhood trauma directly affects children's ability to form healthy attachments and reciprocal relationships. This seemed most prevalent in the stories that mothers shared about their daughters. Mothers typically entered into their parenting role with unvoiced expectations around what their relationship with their child would look like and felt disillusioned when the expectations weren't met.

Heather and John had one biological son when they decided to adopt two sisters who at the time were six and eight. Heather struggled early on when she realized the girls were not looking to her as their mom. They'd had a mom before and had female caregivers in the orphanage. "Dad became a superhero," Heather said. "Me, they put up with. I had to work and struggle to be the woman/mom in their life. I had expectations of kids who'd say, 'Mommy, Mommy, Mommy,' but that wasn't the case at all with our girls. They didn't want anything to do with me. I felt attached, they didn't. In general, there hasn't been a lot of physical affection. I never thought that would be the case. Nevertheless, I'm still determined to love them."

Nora Williams had a heart for adoption for many years but understood that she couldn't press her husband, Landon, on the subject. Instead, she prayed and waited to see what God would do. The Williamses went on to have four biological children and were in a season of launching their kids into adulthood when Landon traveled to Ukraine on a mission trip. While in Ukraine he worked with orphans and at-risk kids at a rehab center, and through that experience God changed his heart. Landon returned to the US and told his wife he was ready to pursue adoption.

Through a hosting program, the Williams family welcomed a thirteen-year-old boy named Vlad into their home, and they felt an instant connection. Nora developed a close relationship with Vlad through the summer they spent with him and felt confident that he was meant to be a part of their family. Nearly a year later, the Williamses traveled to Ukraine to adopt Vlad and were eager to have him join their family permanently. But, as reality set in back in their midwestern home, the family faced unexpected challenges. Vlad began to experiment with drugs and alcohol and make friends in the wrong places. The Williamses kept reaching out, but it seemed to them that Vlad was more interested in independence than in family.

"I don't think I really considered that our son could reject us," Nora said. "I thought of everything—I thought of the path he was on that could have led to prison or addictions or other troubles, but I never thought he would actually reject us as parents. I never thought, 'Wow, you could bring a child to America, love him and integrate him, and then he could decide he didn't want to be a part of a family and reject you.'"

As Nora spoke about the pain of rejection they experienced, Landon added, "I had to recognize that *anything* could happen. I mean, your own biological children can make poor choices and reject you too."

The Williamses never stopped hoping and praying that Vlad would return and embrace the family. They knew he would need help, and at the time of the interview, they were turning a new page with Vlad. He had just finished a rehabilitation and job-training program and was looking forward to returning home.

Another adoptive mom shared how she's grieved over the fact that her relationship with her daughter Katya (adopted at age nine and home for four years at the time of our interview) might not ever be what she'd expected and hoped it would be:

> I don't feel attached because attachment is a two-way thing. I love her. Some days I even like her. I want connection and I think sometimes she wants it too, but she is scared of it. Sometimes I wonder when she's grown and she hits a difficulty if she'll even call us. I think she'd just call a friend instead. I don't have an idealized picture of having a friendship with my daughter when she's an adult, and that's sad because I know I'll have it with my biological daughter.
>
> My husband constantly reminds me that we still have time before she graduates. Who knows, maybe when she's thirty-five it will be different. I haven't lost all hope, but it's not how I pictured it'd be. My main goal now is for her to have a healthy functioning adult life, and somewhere along the way she can find healing and relationships in which she can really connect.
>
> Right now, I'm growing. I'm less hurt. A month and a half ago I had an aha moment—realizing that adopting is not for us at all, it's for the child. I can't

have a relationship with my kids expecting any-thing—from any of them. If there's a reciprocal connection, that's how God intends it to be. In adopting Katya, I was not supposed to expect a great mother-daughter friendship when she got older. That's not something I'm rewarded with just because I adopt. This is about showing her what a family looks like. Hopefully, she'll reciprocate our love someday, but I can't spend all my time on what I hope for in the future. It has to be about her—meeting her where she is and helping her become the healthiest version of herself that she can be.

Redefining Success

One pattern I observed during my interviews was that many families not only were operating out of the "love is enough" mind-set but also went into their adoption with the belief that academic or emotional struggles would be corrected over time through proper attention and focus on bringing the newly adopted child up to speed.

Many of the school-aged adopted children had been labeled with a learning disability in Ukraine and had been placed in institutions for children with similar diagnoses. The methodologies used for diagnosing children with mental disabilities or delays in the Ukrainian orphanage system are outdated and I believe misused. Typically, when children are removed from their homes and placed in institutions, they undergo a battery of tests to determine their cognitive abilities. These tests cannot be very accurate when there's no consideration to the children's stress levels or early childhood trauma.

As a result of the diagnoses that are quickly given to children, the majority spend their formative educational years in institutions where they are not challenged and no adults or educators are attempting to work with them or tailor their schooling to individual learning and development needs. Conversely, the education system in the US excels at providing targeted, IEP (Individualized Education Program) options. However, even the best IEP in the American school system cannot transform children who have suffered from years of understimulation, fetal alcohol syndrome, and other early childhood traumas that affect brain development and function. Education for many adopted children will remain a constant struggle.

Jodi had successfully homeschooled her two biological children for many years when she and her husband added two new daughters through adoption. Jodi assumed that bringing her thirteen- and fourteen-year-old adoptive daughters up to academic speed might take time, but she never considered that some of their delays could be permanent. "I think academically I really thought it would be a piece of cake, especially as a homeschool mom," she said. "I thought we could start at a first-grade level if it was needed and then we could just book right along, and they'd grasp it. And now, three years later, we are still working on telling time. A lot of people told us, 'They'll catch up, it's just a matter of time,' and you kind of want to believe that.

But then as the years go by, you realize how their brains have been impaired by other factors and they may not be able to catch up on some things. That is a reality you have to live with."

Theresa and Henry, another adoptive couple, also didn't recognize or perceive the depth of their adoptive son's delays early on. "I didn't think it would be so difficult to teach him," Theresa said. "I thought that once we crossed the language barrier and he learned English, school would march on as normal like it did for our other kids. That has not been the case. It threw me for a loop that his learning was so delayed. I didn't expect how hard it would be to teach him simple concepts. It's clear there are major gaps in his brain."

In families where the parents had higher degrees or successful careers and the biological children excelled in school, I found it was a struggle when reality set in that an adoptive child might never be capable of performing at age level. This is where understanding the effects of fetal alcohol syndrome and complex trauma on brain development and function is critical. Families that were able to adjust to the abilities and limitations of their children and let go of their own dreams of future academic success fared better than those who fixated on unmet expectations regarding academic acquisition.

As Paul, an adoptive dad of two daughters, shared, "My definition of success has changed a lot. When I first met my daughter before I knew her struggles, I thought, 'Oh she could be a public speaker or advocate for orphans,' because you see the success stories and think, 'My kid could do that!' But then you have to realize, maybe not. God has redefined success for me. What is God's definition of success? That's what I want to be. When I look at Scripture, I see what God says a successful life is. It's not about college education for your kids. For my kids, a job at McDonald's or Home Depot might mean success."

A New Way of Parenting

I've heard counselors say that expectations are premeditated resentments. The more that families can identify their expectations going into the adoption process and learn to let go of them, the better equipped they will be as they transition into a new family unit.

One adoptive father explained his process well:

> Somewhere along the way, my paradigm switched to be more focused on their perspective than my own. I mean, what a traumatic thing: here are some strangers, go live with them in America! And we were expecting them to conform to us and asking them to trust us. I started to see things differently. We had all the resources. We had a choice. They didn't. When you consider this, the fact that you gain any family ground at all is miraculous. I had to come to the place where I could see that my notion of "normal" was an idol, and normal might not happen, and I had to be okay with that.

While other families I spoke with have similarly gotten to the place where they've let go of expectations about what their relationship with their child should look like, some are still grieving the death of a dream. As I sat with adoptive families in city after city, on their couches instead of mine, in their hometowns and not the foreign context of Ukraine where we first met, I heard fewer platitudes and saw more raw emotions. Families spoke freely of fewer mountaintops and more valleys. But in the midst of the hard, I also heard stories of hope and witnessed tremendous resiliency.

After raising seven biological children, Michael and Linda Newman adopted a Ukrainian sibling set who were thirteen and fourteen at the time of the adoption. The Newmans added these children to the mix of their few remaining teens at home. With so much parenting experience, a couple like the Newmans seemed well equipped to handle the nuances of teen adoption. Like many parents, they went into adoption thinking, *We know how to parent; therefore, we have something to offer these kids.* As a result of this thinking, the Newmans, like many adoptive parents, were surprised when their successful parenting strategies didn't prove effective with their newly adopted children. They quickly discovered they'd have to try new tactics if they were going to effectively navigate the complexities of their relationship with their new children.

"All our bio kids had unique journeys and personalities, and we felt like we were equipped for this challenge," Linda said. "We'd dropped expectations for anything ideal because of the bumps we had in the road with our other kids, and we always saw how God worked. We felt like we could enter into this adoption understanding it would be challenging and difficult. But I literally felt like my toolbox was completely empty. I was like, 'Seriously God? I still have this much to learn?' I'd parented all these different styles of kids already and I felt like I had to start all over. . . . It has been so humbling."

Linda's lifeline was reaching out to other adoptive parents and attending a conference that let her know she was not alone in this journey. Through these connections she gained the understanding that she still had a lot to learn about her children's brains that would help her and her husband lovingly parent them.

From this posture of prayerful humility, families like the Newmans are learning to die to their expectations and instead embrace a new way of interacting with their children. Most can look back at the growth and lessons learned and see the ways that they and their children have changed for the better. In many cases, it is evident to me how the trials that could have broken them instead somehow made them stronger.

For Reflection or Group Discussion

1. Describe your version of "rose-colored glasses" in terms of adoption.

2. What are your thoughts about relationship reciprocity with an adopted child? If you have adopted, what does your relationship with your adopted child(ren) look like now compared to what you expected before the adoption? *I expected + to be sweeter, closer, affectionate, but its not at all because of me.*

3. If you were a parent prior to adopting, how do you think your style of parenting might have to change or adapt after adopting? What methods would still work with the adopted child(ren)?

4. What are/were the biggest expectations you had that you had to let go of in adoption? *that he would be sincere and grateful that I would love him like I love my daughters*

Are We There Yet?

Entitlement, Attachment, and Gratitude

We wanted to make up for the lost years we didn't have with them—all the birthdays, all the Christmases. But looking back, we gave our girls more than we should have.

—ADOPTIVE MOTHER

B ecause of what Hollywood has instilled in our culture, generally when people think of adopting kids from an orphanage, visions of rescuing abandoned children longing for forever families come to mind. One mother shared, "When we first adopted our fourteen-year-old son, people would come up to us and say, 'Oh wow, he must be *so grateful!*' Well, they would either say that or they'd look horrified that we adopted a teen! People's views of adoption are so varied."

Some families do experience elements of what others might perceive as "dream" adoptions. Roughly half of the parents I interviewed said their adopted children regularly expressed appreciation on multiple levels about being in a family and having their needs provided for. These families celebrated this positive aspect of their experience.

Tammy and her husband, Brad, adopted eight-year-old Tanya from a special-needs orphanage in central Ukraine in 2012. Tanya, who had cerebral palsy and hydrocephalus, had spent most of her life in a room in an orphanage designated for children confined to beds. She had never been outside the orphanage walls.

Tammy had visited the orphanage the year before, and after meeting this bright, blue-eyed girl, she couldn't get Tanya's face out of her mind. Tammy left Ukraine with a deep sense that her family needed to adopt Tanya. Thankfully, Tammy's husband agreed. Once the adoption was completed and Tanya arrived in America, she underwent extensive surgeries and procedures to meet some of her most critical medical needs. Though there was once hope that she'd gain some mobility, this was not to be. To meet Tanya is to be drawn in by her sweet spirit. One doesn't leave Tanya's presence unchanged.

I spent two days with this family, and what struck me more than anything was Tanya's ability to verbalize her gratitude and joy. She was always smiling, always offering a word of encouragement. Her mom shared:

> She used to tell me several times a week, "I *love* my mommy. I *love* my daddy. I *love* my siblings." She'd go through all our names and just express her love. Every day when I got in the car to take the kids to school, she asked how her brother was because she

knew he was having a rough time at school. She doesn't have any discontent or jealousy where her siblings are concerned. I tell my kids they need to recognize what a gift it is to be loved so completely by their sister. When she first came home, she talked about *detsky dom* (children's home) all the time. She'd say, "At *detsky dom* I ate soup every day. But at home there's no more soup, no more shots, now my mommy and daddy love me." She really understood the dramatic transformation that took place in her life. I know many families struggle with adopted kids who aren't grateful, so I try not to broadcast this a lot. I recognize we're not the norm. Physically, Tanya is difficult to care for, but emotionally she's a dream of a child, and we're so grateful for her.

Hearing stories like this one and seeing Tanya flourish in her new home remind me why I advocate for children to be in families. Still, for the other half of the parents I interviewed, the sense of entitlement they encountered in their children was something they weren't prepared for. Some admitted that they'd held on to a vision of Orphan Annie, with their child gratefully receiving all they had to offer; thus, they were surprised by a lack of appreciation for the blood, sweat, tears, and money they'd invested in the adoption.

Rebecca Jensen remembers telling her biological children, "These kids all just want moms and dads. Just think: we can give them a family, and they'll be so grateful!" Now, a decade later, she recognizes how naive her concept of "rescuing" children was. "Once our new children were here and our biological kids saw how ungrateful and entitled they acted, with great sarcasm they said, 'Yes, they *clearly* wanted a family, Mom!' I never did any of this for a thank-you, but I will say it was hard when my adopted kids had an attitude of, 'You owe me.' "

Heather, who brought her daughters home at the ages of six and eight, said that, at first, she wanted to give them all the good things they'd lacked, but she didn't realize the backlash this could have.

> They'd only been home a couple months when we had our first Christmas as a family. We did the same thing we'd done every year when it had been just our son: we gave them three gifts because, hey, if it was good enough for Jesus, it should be good enough for our kids.
>
> We got things we thought they'd like, but when we got done opening the gifts, the girls acted like, "That's it? Where's the rest of it?" They had a sense of entitlement that seemed very strange. Our daughters, who had nothing before we adopted them, wanted everything, and our son, who had everything, was fine with the littlest thing we gave him. In general, they didn't like anything we gave them; everything we thought they'd want was the complete opposite.

Seven years later, I will say entitlement is still an issue. I was expecting the orphan I saw in the movies—the humble, lowly child, grateful for anything—but they were nothing like this. We gave them everything, and they *still* wanted more.

Nathan and Becky, already parents of four biological children when they adopted fourteen-year-old Dima, admitted they didn't foresee some of the attitudes their son would have, nor his expectations about what they could provide. "I just thought he'd be really grateful and appreciative," shared Becky. "I didn't anticipate his victim mentality and strong sense of entitlement. Early on he asked if we'd send him to a specialized soccer school because his dream was to be a soccer star. I had to explain to him, 'We didn't adopt you to send you away to some school; we want you to be part of this family.' I also made a comment about it being expensive. His response was something like, 'All you think about is money.' I was blown away."

The Role Attachment Plays

It's clear that these parents were surprised by the attitudes their children were expressing, but were they missing a deeper factor that was possibly playing a role in their children's behavior? On the surface, it may appear that kids who demonstrate a sense of entitlement are quite attached to things instead of people, and while this may be true for some, it's not the case with others.

Several years ago, I was helping with an adoption, and the parents commented on how generous they thought their adopted daughter was. This was because of all the personal belongings she was willing to give to her classmates as she left the orphanage. After the conversation, I thought more about the comment and about my interactions with other kids in orphanages over the years and realized that something else might be at play in these moments of perceived generosity.

I remember countless times being at orphanages in my early years in Ukraine and having kids give me random toys so I would "remember them." At first I thought this was very sweet and generous, but over time I started to realize that the behavior was predictable, even down to the exact phrase the kids would use. Typically, the offering was followed by the question, "And what will you give me to remember you?" I would quickly look through the possessions I had with me and try to find a little trinket to leave with the child to ensure that there had been a mutual exchange.

As I saw this little orphanage ritual play out over the years, I began to understand that many of these children gave their things away simply because they placed no value on them. Think about possessions you value. Perhaps you value a family heirloom or a child's first piece of artwork or a gift your spouse gave you on an important anniversary. Even if you consider yourself a minimalist, chances are you own a few things that would be difficult for you to part with because they're sentimental. Likely, you hold an attachment to the person who gave you the item or special memories surrounding the object itself. Your attachment to others *creates* an attachment with objects.

In contrast, kids who have grown up in an institution lack many of these relational bonds, and therefore it is difficult for them to attach meaning or value to items they receive. Something I gave them to "remember me" could very well be given to the next visitor passing through in a couple of weeks. Over time, I began to understand that their few possessions were simply a means of exchange, an attempt to make a connection in the best way they knew how.

Watching the way many kids in orphanages interact with possessions and observing these same kids in interpersonal situations has led me to make a profound connection between a child's ability to attach to an adoptive family and the child's ability to express gratitude or value material possessions in a healthy way. If you spend much time in the adoption world, you'll hear a lot on the topic of attachment. When a parent consistently meets a baby's needs over time, a circle of attachment builds. Baby cries, the parent offers food or changes a diaper, baby is soothed, baby falls asleep. When that cycle repeats again and again, the attachment between child and parent solidifies. When children don't have their basic needs met at an early age or the response is inconsistent, that bond is not created, and, as a result, these children are likely to struggle with trusting other adults to meet basic needs.[1]

I've observed that kids who have a weak attachment to their adoptive families are the ones most likely to lack appreciation for the things they receive. Conversely, in homes where children display healthy attachment toward their adoptive parents, they usually express less entitlement and more gratitude.

I discussed these observations with Evelyn, an adoptive mother of three girls with physical disabilities who integrated well into their new family. Together we explored the importance of kids attaching after joining their adoptive families and the role that attachment plays before a child is even born. Research shows that the nine months of development in the womb are crucial for healthy attachment to continue after birth. A study for the Association for Psychological Science revealed that while in the womb, a baby picks up signals from the mother, including her mental and emotional state. Those messages and signals can be positive or negative. A baby can sense the stresses and adversities the mother experiences and even her signals as to whether the pregnancy is wanted or unwanted.[2]

Sadly, for an adopted child, this in utero period of time and the first two years of life are difficult to gather information about. In most cases inferences can be made only through observing how the child adapts and develops later.

Evelyn shared that one of the factors that could have enabled her three daughters to attach well is that their mothers were likely unaware of the girls' disabilities prior to birth. She conjectured that the birth mothers may very well have been healthy women who were forming healthy attachments with the babies growing inside them. The mothers of these children might have had desired pregnancies and expected healthy babies. Only upon giving birth and discovering the disability would they have made the painful decision to relinquish a child. Usually this decision would be encouraged by family members or doctors because in Ukraine and many other developing countries, raising a child with special needs or disabilities is extremely difficult. Little value is placed on children with disabilities by Ukrainian society at large, and therefore services and support are difficult to come by or simply nonexistent. As Evelyn has observed how her three girls have attached and adapted well in comparison to other adopted children in her community, she's felt the environment they likely experienced in the womb was a key factor at play.

Understanding the negative impact on children who didn't develop secure attachments to their mothers in the womb and then encountered more adversity in their first years of life helps us grasp why some children attach better than others. Knowing as much about a child's history as possible can provide essential clues as to why a child may or may not be able to express emotions, show attachment, and demonstrate appreciation for being brought into a family.

Too Much Too Fast

The impulse of many families is to lavish their kids with what they perceive the kids lacked in the orphanage. Families think of all the missed birthdays and Christmases, and there's a sense of wanting to make sure the newly added children have all the same opportunities and possessions as other children their age. I have rarely seen this strategy produce positive results. In fact, I have observed that adopted kids whose new parents gave them a large number of material possessions right away tended to struggle more with attachment, entitlement, and feeling appreciation for those gifts. Gift giving might be the love language of a parent, or a way to demonstrate care, and this may work well with children who have developed secure attachments (like biological children). But excessive gift giving without the foundation of a healthy relationship can hinder attachment for children who come into a family through adoption.

I have long been fascinated with studying World War II and the Holocaust. One piece of this history that has always haunted me is the number of concentration camp survivors who died shortly after liberation because they were overfed. When the body experiences severe starvation, the gastrointestinal system shuts down and forgets how to digest food. Giving the body too much too soon and the wrong kind of food can lead to severe diarrhea. To a starving person who is already experiencing dehydration, this can mean death.[3] Some emaciated individuals who managed to make it to the end of the war died as a result of being given small bits of chocolate by their foreign liberators. Of course, the intention of the liberating troops was not to harm the Holocaust survivors. They were moved with compassion to do something, to respond and provide what had been lacking. But sadly, sometimes the best intentions can be detrimental when we don't understand the possible impact.

Dave, a dad of two teens in California said, "It's kind of like someone winning the lottery. You hear about people who come from nothing and live in a trailer and then they win the lottery and go broke. It's too much too fast, they don't know how to manage it. Looking back, we gave our kids more than we should have."

Danielle is the mother of several adopted children and was connected with a local adoptive community when she brought her children home. Early on she noticed a difference in how kids were adapting based on the type of home they were adopted into. "I observed that some of the kids who struggled the most after their adoption were those who were adopted into more affluent homes. They seemed to be given too much too quickly and nothing brought them happiness. I saw more successful adaptation in the kids who were adopted into families with limited means. Kids seemed to do better when they had less."

For example, many adopted children and teens were given full access to smartphones or laptop computers and social media accounts within weeks or months of coming home. Due to their kids' age, parents felt they had to keep up with the status quo of the other teens their kids were interacting with in school or the families' biological children. But other families made a firm decision not to allow their adopted children access to unsupervised technology, and some chose to eliminate access to technology nearly altogether. It seemed that parents who chose to home-school for at least a year dealt with fewer demands from a child or teen wanting access to a cell phone. I believe this was largely because the kids weren't comparing themselves to their peers. Even though the tactics can appear strict to some, attachment and bonding clearly increased when the focus on technology and material possessions decreased.

It's also good to keep in mind that children who have a background of trauma and struggle with attaching can be at greater risk in using technology. A recent study by the Christian Alliance for Orphans found that children and adolescents who have weak attachments may use technology, particularly social media, to "connect" with others, and that connection will not always be healthy and can provide a false bond. Children with unhealthy attachments may not be able to discriminate between "safe" and "unsafe" people, which in turn can compromise their well-being online.[4] Though kids did not typically react positively to their parents restricting or limiting technology use, when that time was redirected toward bonding with the family, the positive results were noticeable.

Megan and Henry Davis have three daughters, who were between the ages of twelve and sixteen at the time of our interview. The Davises said they have worked hard to quash any sense of entitlement. "We tried very hard to keep our girls' world very small and focused on not having a lot of material things and keeping our family close. Thankfully, we can walk through a store and none of our kids will ask for anything. . . . We show them by example that we're trying to be generous and serve others and that it's not all about us and what we deserve. We have ancient phones and older furniture. We have worked to model simplicity to them, and they seem to be seeing it and learning."

The Adoptee's Perspective

As I sat with families across the United States and listened to their stories, one thing that stood out to me was their bravery. But it was the older adoptees' bravery in particular that made the biggest impact on me. Somewhere between the ages of thirteen and sixteen, these young people had made the decision to entrust their safety and security to adults they barely knew. Whether the underlying motivation was a better life outside Ukraine or to gain family connection, their decision to leave all they had ever known was incredibly courageous.

Recently I made the decision to leave my life in Ukraine and move back to the United States. After almost fifteen years of making Ukraine home, it was emotional, and at times painful, to let go of the land where I had built a life. Today, I am attempting to plant roots in a homeland that has become quite foreign to me. As I've faced the task of saying goodbye to my life in Ukraine and begun to find my bearings in the US, I have developed deeper empathy for the children whose stories are represented in this book. I already know the language and have a network of family and friends to reconnect with, and yet the transition has still been challenging for me. As I made my own tearful departure from Ukraine, I realized I'd never fully comprehended the magnitude of the transition these young adoptees made, nor the depth of their losses.

It is difficult to start over—even if the process brings with it the promise of family. And yet I've seen older adoptees master the English language, graduate high school, get jobs, enroll in colleges or universities, and attempt to figure out how to be a part of a family. Most have come to realize that it isn't the glamorous picture they'd imagined. Some have been more successful in the world's eyes than others, but in my eyes they are all heroes for taking a leap of faith for a fresh start.

Alex, a bright and jovial eighteen-year-old young man who had been adopted four-and-a-half years earlier, shared candidly about the struggles he had in transitioning into his new family.

> I had to start over when I came here. It was really hard at first to learn English, and it was difficult to trust people. Knowing that I had parents and siblings who loved me was a great feeling, but everything was weird here. I had times when I missed my friends and Ukraine so much that I wanted to go back. Ukraine is still part of me. I'm never going to be fully American. In fact, I don't think I've ever felt fully at home in America. I've had to make a lot of changes in myself to be here, and there are a lot of things I'll always compare to Ukraine. I know this is my "home" now, but I never really consider it as my home-home, if you know what I mean. But

I also don't know how I'll feel when I go back to Ukraine someday. Perhaps after I'm here longer, it will feel different.

When I asked Alex what his best advice would be for a kid being adopted to the US, he said, "Forget everything you think about America or what people have told you. Before I came here, I envisioned a lot of things, but it wasn't the way I expected it to be at all. Be open to anything, and eventually you'll get used to it."

About halfway through my travels I was given the privilege of hearing from another adoptee who was learning about trust and gratitude. Adopted at the age of eight, Maria admitted that her transition to living in a family had not always been easy. I shared Thanksgiving with Maria's family, and after the evening meal, everyone gathered in the living room and shared what they were most grateful for.

When it was Maria's turn to speak, she expressed that "[Being adopted], sometimes you have an identity crisis, and sometimes you think, 'Who am I?' and 'What were my parents like?' I have adoptive parents I'm kind of like, but I'm curious what good traits I got from my biological parents—and even which bad traits I got," she said with a laugh. "But I am thankful that I was adopted into my family and that they showed me what it means to love and follow Jesus. I've changed a lot these last seven years. I'm learning to trust. Trusting in God is sometimes really hard because sometimes you don't know if He's there. I have to remember that I'm not in control, and I have to sit back and watch Him do His thing. I know that God has a lot planned for me. . . . [And] I'm really grateful that I've been growing closer with my family."

As I listened to Maria share her story, my eyes filled with tears. I'd sat with her parents just the day before, listening to the ups and downs of parenting Maria as they watched her take some steps forward and then several steps back. They shared with me how they were learning to lower their expectations around an adopted child being grateful and what that would even look like in practice. Yet here we were, observing their daughter making strides toward healing and growing in gratitude and trust, openly sharing about it on Thanksgiving in front of the whole family. It was a Thanksgiving I know I'll never forget.

I heard another encouraging story from Ethan and Brenda Lewis, who adopted their son, Nick, when he was thirteen. They had no biological children and for a season had explored foster care in the US, but they decided to pursue adoption from Ukraine after they met Nick through a hosting program. Both Ethan and Brenda felt they were fairly well prepared for adoption because of the reading they did and training they received, but they hadn't anticipated some of the attitudes they would encounter in their son.

At the time of my interview with Ethan and Brenda, Nick was eighteen and had been part of their family for five years. Nick had just returned home after spending three months living with his girlfriend's family, where he'd been able to escape the rules and standards his parents were placing on him. But hearts were softening between them, and Nick chose to move back home. He agreed to go to counseling, and the family was making progress toward healing after a bumpy past year. They shared one story that struck me as profound. I share it here as a small glimpse into what an adoptee might be processing as they learn to be part of a family.

"A few months back Nick went out and I got in touch with him on the phone. He was really drunk, and he suddenly was saying all these things that he'd never said before," Ethan recalled. "He said, 'I'm so sorry, I really screwed up everything, I'm so ungrateful and you saved me and I'm doing all this to you—What's wrong with me? My own parents rejected me, and *you* came and got me. . . .' He went on and on like that, and on one hand it was horrible . . . [but] it also felt like he was being honest and speaking from his heart. We tried to go back to that moment when he was sober, but he couldn't go there. I think it scared him; his *emotions* scared him. We are hopeful [that] with counseling . . . we can get back to a good place."

As Ethan told this story, I could tell that the words his son shared in that moment on the phone felt like a glimmer of hope. Ethan continued on to say that one night his son stormed out of the house after they'd been arguing. Right after he left, a salesman knocked on the door.

> He asked us if we were Ukrainian because he saw the Ukrainian flag we had outside our house. We said no, but our son was, and we proceeded to share that we'd been having some struggles with

87

him and it had been a hard day. He was from Belarus, so he understood Ukrainian culture. He went on to encourage us, saying that he, too, had gone through a rough period in his life and that there was still hope that our son would pull through. . . . Never before had a salesman come to our door and never again after. We like to think of him as our Belorussian angel. It was exactly the encouragement we needed in that moment.

I recognize that not all parents will ever get to hear their children articulate gratitude or even verbalize their growth. As one mother expressed, "Maybe someday I'll get a thank-you note, but then again, maybe I won't. I know I can't be living for the thank-you note; that's not what this is about." I found that the better families understood where their children had come from and how their history affected their ability to attach and express gratitude, the more these families were able to manage their expectations and watch for opportunities to learn and grow. They had to learn patience—not only with their children but also with themselves as they adapted to the changes in their family.

Alex, the young adoptee quoted earlier, said, "Give your kids time. I think patience is one of the biggest things kids need while they are figuring out how to be in a family. Pushing a kid to do things too fast is not helpful because he's just trying to adapt to all the new things he hasn't done before. It's hard for parents to truly understand what a kid is going through or what he's been through. You feel lost when you first come home. One of the things I appreciate most about my parents is that they didn't push me. They gave me *time*, and it helped."

His mom, Monica, agreed. "Be patient with the process of bonding and developing the relationship. I remember someone telling me, 'The first six months are the hardest,' and then thinking, 'Can someone just put me out for those six months until this is over?' But I had to learn that this is a marathon, not a sprint. Rome wasn't built in a day, and becoming a family doesn't happen in a month or even in a year. You have to undo and redo. If you go in with a savior complex, you're in for it. It will get easier. You will see light at the end of the tunnel eventually, though at times it feels like all you see are trains."

For Reflection or Group Discussion

1. Did you or someone you know enter adoption with expectations that the adopted child would be grateful? How were those expectations met or unmet?

2. If you have adopted, how did you handle material possessions when your child first came home? Looking back, would you do anything differently? If so, what?

3. How would you correlate the degree to which you see your adopted or biological child attached to you (parents) and the degree to which your child can express sincere gratefulness?

4. Do you think gratitude is important for a person to be healthy? Why or why not?

5. Do you see any parallels between your gratefulness (or lack thereof) to God and your adopted child's expressions of gratefulness to you?

5

Rough Road Ahead

Parenting When the Feelings Aren't There

My friend helped me remember that love is not a feeling. When we act against what we feel and choose love—that is really love.

—ADOPTIVE MOTHER

Kathleen and Andrew Walker adopted eight-year-old Natasha in 2014. Andrew describes the moment he saw Natasha for the first time as exceeding all his expectations. "I wasn't expecting a love-at-first-sight kind of scenario, but that's what it was," he said. He remembers waiting in the orphanage's formal seating area for her to come to them for the first time. "I could see this blonde little girl rounding the corner. As I saw her coming down the short hallway, I was done for. . . . We all stood up and headed out into the main corridor of the orphanage. I took three or four steps, and before I realized it, she turned, looked at me, grabbed my hand, and hauled me off to show me around the orphanage like she knew what was happening. There were no doubts in my mind, and there was no going back."

As Kathleen and Andrew told their adoption story, they finished each other's sentences, remarked on how God's fingerprints were on all aspects of the process, and teared up as they recounted the beautiful way the Lord led them to Natasha. They have had their share of behavioral struggles with their daughter over her four years at home, and our conversation revealed that she has challenges to overcome. But her parents' feelings of love and attachment came across as consistent and steadfast, and I believe this attachment is what helps them to keep pressing on in the harder moments that adoption presents.

Many families I spoke with initially heard beautiful stories like this and were even motivated to adopt by statements like, "I love her as if she were my own." Some of these same families were left spinning, however, when they didn't experience those deep, loving emotions toward their own adopted child. I heard from many parents who found themselves blindsided by their sheer lack of feelings, a tough reality that they never anticipated.

Dana and Aaron adopted four-year-old Mark in 2011. Having several older biological children, they assumed that adding a younger child to the mix would be natural, with only minor adjustments. "We thought we would love him just like our other kids. We thought he'd have a problem attaching and thought we were very well read on the subject," Dana said. "We never thought *our* lack of bonding would be an issue. I felt like some other person had taken over my body. . . . In my mind it had become romanticized that I'd run to him and want to scoop him up—and I didn't have that feeling. I was so broadsided by the lack of attachment and remember thinking, 'What is wrong with me? *He* is the one who's supposed to be having the problem.' I kept asking myself, 'Why am I struggling so much in loving this child?' "

A Sensitive Topic

There is no getting around the fact that this is a sensitive topic, one often laced with self-condemnation and guilt. No parents pursue adoption thinking they won't love the child who comes into their family, but the reality is that many factors play into feelings of love or lack of love. The child's temperament, behavior, and attachment style, as well as the parent's personality, attachment style, and expectations, are all part of the mix.

Early on in my journey, I discovered that parents' lack of feelings for an adopted child was a topic not adequately addressed in the adoption community, and therefore one that contributed to feelings of isolation. Many parents shared they didn't feel like they had a safe place to express their emotions, for fear of their children ever knowing. They also feared being judged by others.

I want to come up with some nice way of talking about all of this, but the truth is, it's very complicated. People are complex. Every couple comes into adoption with both assets and deficits that directly affect parenting styles and the ability to attach to a child. And, as discussed earlier, children from an institutionalized background have different levels of wounding that correlate with their ability to integrate and attach to any family, let alone one from a different culture. On my long drives between states, I would sometimes play a game in my head where I would hypothetically swap certain kids into other families (there were some *really* long driving days). How would this child have done in that family, or would that family have fared better with this other child? Would that parenting style have worked better for Sasha? Would the Jones family have been a more therapeutic home for Inna? Would Kerri have been able to attach better to a child like Dasha? Thankfully, no one gave me an opportunity to put my theories to the test, and all the kids remain where I found them!

From my observation and experience, international adoptions as a whole do not have great procedures or methodologies for matching children to families. A typical situation in Ukraine is that you see a child's picture, go visit the child for several hours, then decide if you want to adopt said child. One father even compared adoption to an arranged marriage. This is why many families choose to go the route of hosting a child before committing to an adoption. In all honesty, however, hosting a child is not a fail-safe method for ensuring a bond with the child once the adoption is complete. During hosting, not only is there a language barrier but both parents and children are typically on their best behavior, and sometimes hosting serves as more of a honeymoon experience than an accurate take on reality. Some families I spoke with who had hosted children and felt a sense of connection at first went on to struggle with a lack of emotion once the children came home.

Matt and Shannon Burke experienced an interesting contrast in their level of emotional attachment to the two ten-year-olds they adopted. They had two daughters, ages four and six at the time of the family's adoption. They'd hosted ten-year-old Ana through a summer program, fallen in love with her, and committed to her adoption. As they moved forward in the paperwork process, they learned of another boy in the same orphanage who needed a family. Filled with compassion and the thought that they surely could "take one more," the Burkes agreed to adopt ten-year-old David as well. Now, four years after bringing their two children home, the Burkes feel very attached to their daughter Ana but still struggle with their lack of feelings of love and attachment toward their son.

Shannon shared candidly about the conflicting and varying feelings she experiences. "Ana can make me so angry, but I feel like she's mine, and I'd do anything for her. I love her completely. But then there's David. I've gone through moments when I say, 'Okay, I'm the caregiver, and as long as I'm the caregiver, I can do this.' Honestly, I don't know how to be a mom to him, and he doesn't know how to be a son. I find that I often resent him because he is never content. He wants to be entertained all the time. He thought he was coming to

Disneyland, but that's not who I am. It's a continual struggle."

Matt, the father, also admitted that he's still not very attached to his son. "I was super close with my own dad," Matt shared. "He wanted to spend time with me and take me places, so I have this idea of what a father-son relationship could be. I don't feel like that dad to David; life with him just seems forced. I want to feel like a family, yet I don't like one of my kids a lot of the time, and that's hard. It may never be the way it's 'supposed' to look, but I keep pressing in."

Rachel and Kyle had no children when they adopted two toddler-age siblings. Rachel struggled when she didn't feel herself attaching to her new children. "I had so many expectations for how hard it'd be for them to attach to us, and in many ways it was. But I had no idea how hard it'd be for me to attach to *them*," she said. "We did all the trainings, we read all the books, we watched the videos, and we never felt that anyone talked about parents not attaching to their children. I wasn't prepared for that."

Through tears, Rachel continued, "I struggle because there is great guilt and shame over the fact that when Lily gets hurt, I don't have this overwhelming sense that I want to run and hold her. . . . Instead I'm aware that I'm telling myself, 'You are her mom—go to her.' " It has been difficult for Rachel to make sense of her lack of emotional connection to her adopted children, which has been amplified since adding more children to their family biologically.

Jessica, a mother of two adopted sons, was similarly troubled at her lack of emotional connection to one of her sons who was diagnosed with extreme reactive attachment disorder and, as a result, has brought significant disorder to what was once a peaceful home.

> My expectation was that I would come to love my kids as a natural mother would love her own biological children. But when I was not feeling those natural maternal feelings that come more easily with my other children, I felt a lot of guilt. I doubted if I was even a Christian. I was very aware of my lack of love, and I struggled a lot with it. I remember being out on a run one day and thinking to myself, "Would I be sad if he died?" It took me a little while, and I finally realized that yes, I would be sad if he was gone. But what bothered me was that I actually had to *think* about it. It's taken time for me to learn that even if the "feelings" of love never come, I can still walk in obedience.

Rachel echoed these thoughts. "I see my own sin and preference for what's natural. But then I see that God loves us simply because He loves us. I don't love because my kids are lovely—I love because God first loved me. I admit, I have struggled in my faith over this. Our adoption has illuminated for me what favoritism is and how the Bible gives examples of parents who preferred certain children and it destroyed their families. This has helped me realize that love is a choice, not a feeling. I recognize that I can choose love daily, and I pray that at some point we can attach."

Love Deposits

While interviewing families, I was intrigued and surprised by the observation that a lack of attachment to a child didn't always correlate with the level of difficult behavior exhibited by that child. The majority of the parents I spoke with who were struggling with their feelings of emotional connection were not parenting children with extremely difficult behaviors. One mother even commented that her child was not unruly or defiant but generally agreeable, which made her lack of emotional attachment that much harder for her to process. In contrast, parents who were dealing with children who did exhibit more challenging behaviors didn't seem to withdraw from their children if they had stronger emotional attachments to them. It was the emotional connection that allowed them to keep pressing on in the most difficult times. I found these situations to be similar to how parents respond to biological children who rebel. Despite frustration and sometimes infuriation with the behavior, their deeper attachment keeps them connected.

One mother, Linda, shared that one of her biggest revelations was in understanding why she was so quick to react to the behaviors of her adopted children and why she had a hard time feeling emotionally connected. She received a book at an adoption conference that described the relationship between any parent and child as a bank.

When you have biological kids, they do things that are hard to deal with. They are naughty when they are little and misbehave, but they're also constantly making love deposits in your bank. They snuggle up to you and do cute things, and as a result they fill up your love bank. So when those same children yell at you at a later date, they are withdrawing from that bank—but at least you have a bank.

The hardest thing about adopting older children is that there is no bank to start with. Suddenly they begin withdrawing, without depositing, and you get empty pretty fast. That was the best word picture to describe what I was experiencing. After that was explained I no longer felt the weight of guilt and shame over struggling to connect with my adopted kids. It was just a reality: we don't have that history; we don't have those banks. This understanding helped me give myself grace. I've always loved them and can see them as my children, but when things were hard, it felt different with them than with my biological kids. Now I have the words to explain why.

Cara, another adoptive mom, brought up the need for grace as well. "I have to continually remind myself to give myself grace in my parenting. Because God has. I think, 'Why are you withholding something from yourself that God has freely poured out? Don't be stingy with yourself. You can't fix everything. You can try. You will try. And some of it will stick. Celebrate what sticks and stop bashing your head against the wall when it doesn't.' "

Grieving What Was

Many families revealed another aspect of the lack of attachment to their adopted child: the unexpected pain and grief they've experienced over the loss of their previous nuclear family. One father explained, "I wish someone had told me that I was trading in the family I had for a different one. I wasn't prepared for that, but that's what happened overnight." Another parent shared similar feelings as she expressed her deep grief over her lack of emotion toward her newly adopted child. "I missed the simplicity and predictability of my old life and found myself wanting to put him to bed early, just to have time with the rest of the family and pretend like things were as they had been before the adoption."

Mindy, a mother who brought an eight-year-old boy into the mix of three biological kids, shared with me how the grief she experienced took her by surprise:

> I grieved over losing my original family, and I felt ashamed and guilty. After all, we *chose* to do this. But I missed what our family had looked like and realized it would never be the same. I was thinking he would assimilate into our family, and instead we had to find a new normal. I was crying out to God, "I don't know what to do." I was faced with a dark part of me that I hadn't realized was there. I was

angry and resentful and didn't want to deal with those emotions. I was often overly critical of my adopted son. My other kids would even point out to me how I was treating him differently and picking on him for certain things.

I eventually got counseling about this. I had to learn that I couldn't parent him like I parented my other kids. I had to be okay with the fact that I was being called to the principal's office for trouble he was getting into. I'd never experienced that with my other kids. Looking back, I would say to myself, "Get yourself into counseling a lot earlier, girl!" I'd tell myself to not let shame and guilt get in the way of opening up, talking to people, and receiving help. I should have looked for more support, but at that time I was so overwhelmed and felt like I had to keep it all together.

Sabrina, who adopted Vera at age ten and already had three biological children, echoed Mindy's feelings. "Adoption definitely changes the trajectory of a family. And we knew that would be the case, but I don't think I expected or understood the grieving process I would have to go through. I wish someone had told me, 'It's normal, and it's okay,' because it caught me totally off guard. It's hard to put it into words for someone who hasn't been through it, but the grief is very real. I remember times when I wanted to take the other three kids and do something with them alone, just to recreate what was." Sabrina told me that she now makes a point to bring up this subject when she meets prospective adoptive mothers.

Pressing On in Hope

All these aspects of bonding or lack of bonding between adoptive parents and their kids factor into the emotions that a family—both parents and children—might feel on any given day. These are the realities of adoption that often get overlooked or glossed over. Yet, as I talked with families about the pain and sadness surrounding a lack of emotional love, it was evident that those who struggled in this area had not given up hope. I witnessed how people were working toward not letting their emotions dictate their actions and choosing love when the feelings weren't there.

Sylvia and Rick are in full-time ministry and had three biological children, ages eight, eleven, and fourteen, when they adopted three more children, ages four, six, and seven. When asked about how they processed the transition in their family, Sylvia shared, "It was such a whirlwind, I didn't even know what I was feeling most of the time. I was just trying to keep them alive, safe, and then in bed at the end of the day. I was lucky if I could keep everyone from screaming and crying. At times I thought, 'What have I done?' Prior to adoption I wasn't a crier, but adoption made me into one. I cried more in those first two years post-adoption than I had in my whole life."

Yet even in their hardest moments, both Rick and Sylvia could not deny that God had called them to adopt. "When

I'd start grieving and be tempted to think it would be easier if we didn't have these kids, I'd remind myself that obedience doesn't come without sacrifice, and then I'd think, 'Where would these children be if they weren't in my home? That's not a good picture. No, this is where they are supposed to be. Maybe this isn't picture-perfect, but that's okay.' Gradually I could take myself through the cycle and get back to doing what was right."

As a follower of Christ, this aspect of adoption both humbles and challenges me as I reflect on my relationship with the Lord. I recognize that our daily walk with Jesus will not be sustained if it's built only on warm, fuzzy feelings. Instead, we find the strength to keep walking forward based on what we know to be true, even when our feelings don't match. It's easy to say that love is not a feeling, but I truly believe that as we continue to walk out that truth in our daily lives, we, like these adoptive couples, are offering a sacrifice of praise to God that brings joy to His heart.

For Reflection or Group Discussion

1. In what ways do you relate to the parents quoted early in the chapter who shared that they were blindsided by the fact that they were not attaching to their adopted children?

2. In what ways have you struggled with guilt or shame surrounding any lack of feelings toward your adopted child? Do you know someone who has adopted and is struggling with lack of feelings for their child? How can you encourage them?

3. Several mothers in this chapter referenced choosing love when they did not feel emotionally connected to their children. Can you relate? If so, how?

4. In what ways did you grieve the loss of what your family was prior to adoption, if you have adopted?

5. If you have adopted, do you have a safe place to discuss the challenging emotions around your experiences? If so, who do you feel most comfortable sharing with? If not, where might you be able to find support?

6

Did We Leave Anyone at the Gas Station?

Integrating Biological and Adopted Children

I just wanted all the kids to get along so we would feel like a family.

—ADOPTIVE MOTHER

In many ways, biological children in a family approach the adoption journey with the same rose-colored glasses as their parents, only with a childlike filter. Most of the families I interviewed had biological children at the time of adoption. During our conversations, I found that many were not prepared for the disappointments and challenges that often came as a result of trying to merge two sets of children into one family. The impact of adoption on biological children was much greater, and the integration of siblings much harder, than anyone had anticipated.

I found this to be particularly true for biological kids who were under the age of twelve at the time their adopted siblings entered the family. These children tended to be full of positive anticipation for what they expected a new sibling would mean. Clearly, it would involve having a new playmate and friend! They often got behind fundraising efforts and even donated some of their own money. They lived with Christmas morning-like expectations surrounding the arrival of their new sibling(s). But as one mom shared, "My daughter gave her tooth fairy money to bring home her brother, and he came home and stole her bike. The novelty wore off pretty quickly, and [our kids] realized he wasn't going to be nearly as much fun as they thought he'd be."

By getting to stay in the homes of the majority of the families I visited, I was given the opportunity to see family dynamics up close, specifically concerning sibling interactions and relationships. I had many conversations with both adoptive parents and biological children in which I explored the areas that contributed to smoother transitions within families and examined how children who were already in the home adjusted to the addition of adopted siblings from a foreign land.

I remember fondly the time I spent with a sweet family with eight children, half of them adopted and several with special needs. In this family I saw how the biological siblings embraced their roles as helpers and the family unit operated with grace and compassion. They faced some challenges, but there was a clear sense of a culture that said, "We help one another—we are family."

In another home, I chatted with a lovely teenage biological daughter who, in spite of challenges with her adopted siblings, said she couldn't imagine life without them. She was quick to add that life with a small family would be dull and boring.

Yet another teenage biological daughter shared that her adopted siblings have taught her compassion. After watching her parents' journey to help kids gain a family, she hopes to adopt one day as well.

For Jennifer and Robert, who had an eight-year-old biological son and adopted two daughters close to their son's age, integration didn't prove to be a major struggle. They've had their share of challenges with behavior but credit their son and his temperament for making the transition smooth. "He never complained. Not once. They hardly fight. They have healthy competition. He takes ownership in the adoption and will even say, 'When *we* adopted you . . .' because he understands he was a part of it. His attitude is a gift and we recognize that it's not typical."

Other biological children I encountered who'd once been enthusiastic about welcoming a new brother or sister expressed how profoundly disappointed they were when they realized that these new siblings didn't know how to engage in play, stole their things, lied continually, and caused their parents to get angry or sad. A childhood that had once been carefree suddenly became chaotic when a newly adopted sibling introduced unexpected behaviors into the family.

The Larsons already had one son and two daughters when they added two more sons and a daughter through adoption. All three of their biological children were thrilled with the idea of adding siblings, but looking back, the Larsons see how they didn't adequately prepare their children for the integration of the new family members.

"We didn't have any training for how to deal with what it'd be like to integrate two families," explained the father. "The biggest challenge was with our boys. Our son Danny cried with pure joy when he found out he was getting two brothers. Then about a year and a half after we'd been home with the kids and things weren't going so great, Danny said, 'They're *not* my brothers—they'll *never* be my brothers.' I told Danny, 'The Lord is going to have to change that in your heart. The fact is, they *are* your brothers now.' "

Jessica, mother to a six-year-old who struggles with reactive attachment disorder, said that a lot of the grief she experienced around adopting centered on how she saw the behaviors of her biological children changing as a result. "I think everything culminated when I watched my two little kids begin to rage. My adopted son taught my other children how to punch walls and how to scream and kick and flail on the ground like animals, and that brought out a mama bear in me. I thought, 'How dare you mess with my children?' Not that he isn't my child, but he was messing with my biological kids and teaching them behaviors they never had before. In those moments I thought, 'What have I done to my family?' "

I sat with a couple whose adult biological children won't come to family gatherings if their adopted brother is there due to the drama he causes. The couple shared heartbreaking stories of ruined holidays and fractured relationships. In another home, an adult biological son candidly shared his heart about the ways his adopted siblings wreaked havoc on his family, manipulating and emotionally abusing his parents. After the chaos he witnessed in his home growing up, he says he would never consider adopting himself.

In home after home, I saw different scenarios and a variety of ways that parents and biological children figured out (or stumbled through) adapting to life as a new family unit. It became clear that biological kids were either better or bitter as a result of their parents' choice to adopt.

Recognize the Impact of Disrupting Birth Order

Nearly all adoption experts advise parents not to disrupt the birth order in the family. That means if you have a fourteen-year-old, ten-year-old, and eight-year-old, the experts would say you shouldn't adopt a fifteen- or twelve-year-old; instead, you should add a child who is younger than eight. Adoption books will tell you that this is best for the family dynamics and the adopted child's transition.

In Ukraine, primarily older children and sibling sets are available for adoption. This means that most families don't have the opportunity to adopt a younger child that would fit their biological children's birth order. In fact, 62 percent of the families I interviewed did exactly the opposite of what the experts say to do: they changed the birth order of their original family when adopting from Ukraine.

Sylvia Thomas, a mom of three biological and three adopted kids, shared that the initial transition was difficult, and each of her children responded very differently. She surmised that many of their reactions were based on their birth order in the family.

> We lost our youngest son for a while. He was the same age as the oldest child we adopted, and that was hard. He withdrew for a bit. But then as we gave him time and space, he engaged and ended up becoming the most helpful of all our children, taking real ownership in helping the new kids learn the ropes of the family. Our oldest biological daughter was busy with her own life and activities, so I think she was oblivious to a lot of the challenges we were having. In general, what helped our biological kids when it was hard was that they knew why we'd adopted these new siblings—that it was in obedience to God's call. Our kids had prayed for them for years. They understood why we made this decision and that God was in it.

Many parents said that, though they knew there might be challenges as a result of changing the birth order in their home, they chose to believe God was bigger than letting birth order dictate a decision as to whether or not a child got a family. As one mother put it, "We adopted out of birth order because Aslan is not a tame lion." (Read *The Lion, the Witch and the Wardrobe* by C. S. Lewis if that reference is lost on you.)

I am the first to agree that families need to be sensitive to how the Holy Spirit is leading, and He may very well lead them to adopt out of birth order. This was often the case for families who had hosted Ukrainian children or heard a story about a specific child. But after my many observations, my word of caution is this: a calling from God, or even a strong desire to be a family for a child in need, does not mean that a family will be immune to the challenges and potential repercussions that may occur if the natural birth order is disrupted.

Mindy and Kevin's adopted son, Vadim, was just one year younger than their youngest biological child when they brought him home. "Our youngest daughter thought he would be the baby to coddle. He wasn't. He was chatty and loud and created chaos everywhere. So instead she would push him away," Mindy said. "Our oldest daughter reached out to him more, but he pushed her away. In hindsight, I wish I'd drawn out of my other kids how they felt as well. The kids would often say, 'You're always giving attention to Vadim.' He was clingy, nonstop, and never calm. It was hard for them to adjust to him being in our family. Our oldest daughter was able to verbalize to me how hard it was when we brought him home, and this helped her adjust to the disruption over time."

After listening to dozens of adoptive parents and their biological children talk about the challenges surrounding the integration of siblings, I have given much thought to what contributed to the smoothest transitions. I learned a lot from the families who shared what they wish they had done differently, and I appreciated the wisdom they wanted to pass along to other families working toward successful integration. What follows are several of the pearls of wisdom I gleaned from my interviews and observations.

Be Careful Not to Glamorize Adoption

As you can surmise by now, adopting an older child is very different from adding a baby to a family through birth or even adoption. A baby adds a new dynamic and displaces an older child's position in the family, but adopting an older child involves many different and often more challenging nuances.

Parents are wise to have honest conversations with their children before they adopt and avoid glamorizing the addition of new siblings. It's important to talk about the sacrifices that will have to be made, including the extra attention that parents will need to give to this new child. I observed that when parents discussed with their biological children (in an age-appropriate manner) the issues or challenges their adopted siblings could have, the biological kids responded in a more compassionate way. Open conversation also created a foundation for having more discussion when things proved challenging.

Some parents talked about how their biological children were blindsided by grief after an adopted child joined the family. I observed that the emotions children experienced around the loss of their original nuclear family were very similar to what some parents experienced. Therefore, it's wise to prepare biological children for possibly feeling sad after the new child comes home. One mom advised, "Explain [to your bio kids] that it might be a lot of fun at first (maybe or maybe not!), but in time, they might come to miss the way their family was before adopting, and there may be sadness and grief attached to this. Help normalize those feelings. When we told our kids that their sad feelings were okay, we saw them begin to process and work through their emotions."

Give Biological Children Opportunities to Be Heard

"Can we send him back, Mom? He's so mean. You just don't see it."

When a fourteen-year-old Amanda said this, she was trying to get her mom, Becky, to understand her feelings after Amanda's newly adopted teenage brother came into their home.

Becky later acknowledged, "I think when my biological kids were little and were mean to each other, I had a better sense of what was going on. When we brought Dima home, I didn't see what was happening. Both Amanda and Samantha would draw my attention to it and say how mean he was being to them and how I wasn't seeing it. I think he was pretty sneaky about it."

Becky started making a point of having check-ins with her daughters. She'd take the girls out for one-on-one dates and give them a chance to process their feelings about adding a brother to the family.

> I'd have to draw out the emotions of my younger daughter, Samantha, but Amanda would just spew, and I'd let her. But she was also very teachable. So, after she vented for a while, we would talk about it more realistically and would pray about it together and bring God into the situation. Samantha, on the other hand, is still struggling. I think in time she'll see this as a good thing—and there are moments when they have fun together and I see it—but there are a lot of times, like at school, where Dima is a very charming kid and people like him. She sees how he behaves at home, so she doesn't trust him. It's a difficult relationship, but the experiences we have together as a family seem to help. Time helps.

When Carol and Rob Lind added nine-year-old Katya to their family, their three biological kids were anticipating the arrival of the new sister they had been praying for. Katya took the number two spot in the birth order, just slightly younger than the Lind's oldest and slightly older than the second-born. Having been homeschooled for many years, the Lind's biological kids shared a close bond and were best friends and playmates. Carol shared that they were more than ready to welcome a new sister into their

tight-knit family culture and received Katya with arms
open wide.

Our youngest daughter, Emma, wanted a sister so
desperately, but when we brought Katya home it
was a battle from the beginning. Our intention was
for the girls to share a room for a couple of years,
but they lasted together for only a couple of
months. On the first night home, we had this cute
angelic picture of the girls gazing at each other
fondly from their bunk beds, but after that, it was
all downhill. Emma is a very tenderhearted person,
and the way that Katya was treating her was not
good. We knew there would be hard parts to the
transition, but three-and-a-half years later, Katya
still treats the other kids with disdain. She pushes
them away on purpose.

A month ago, our youngest son had this huge
meltdown over how she was treating everyone, and
I let him spill it all out. I said, "I get it, because she
treats me like that too. You can always come to me
and tell me how you feel if you're frustrated."

The next day, I had the three bio kids in the car
and we were driving somewhere, and I said, "You
guys, I know it's hard with Katya, and I know I
should have talked to you about this a long time
ago, but I know you try really hard and I want you
to keep trying. I also want you to know that your

feelings are okay, and it's okay if you're angry or frustrated. I know life is harder now than it was before."

Carol went on to share how the conversation in the car seemed to reconnect her with her biological children after a season of tension. After that, a door opened for better communication with her kids, and she and her husband continued to create time and space for them to discuss how they felt. "I don't think we had the foresight early on to ask how they were doing. Now I can see when they are getting frustrated and can tell them to come talk to me."

Cara and Chad Bower's experience was slightly different. When they added eight-year-old Sam to the mix of their three biological kids, their adopted son slid in between the second and third child in the family. Early on Cara made it a point to check in regularly with her kids about how they were feeling, but as time passed, she began to wonder if that was the best method to help them transition. She decided she needed to create a balance between hearing how they felt and not allowing their negative feelings to take over.

> I often asked my kids, "How do you feel?" They'd express how they felt, and it would break my heart even more, and I'd think, "I've ruined my family and their existence because of this terror living in their house now!"

My kids would say the same prayer at bedtime every night, thanking God for everyone, but one night they were praying and my youngest son left Sam out of the prayer. I asked him, "Why did you leave out your brother?" And he said, "I don't want to talk to God about Sam right now."

Later I read an article that said sometimes you have to put your feelings on the back burner, stop thinking about how you feel, and just do what needs to be done. I thought about this and decided to try this thinking with my kids. "It really doesn't matter how you feel at this point," I said. "All you have to do is work, and you work until it works. It's not *Survivor*; you don't get to vote him off the island. If you're miserable, stop thinking about being miserable until you feel better about it. Put it on the back burner and simmer it, turn it on low, and check it again in six months. We aren't going to have a council meeting just because he's bugging you. That's not how this is going to work." I decided to stop asking my kids how they felt all the time. I would let the topic go for a while and then go back to it with them. And in time I can say that it got better.

Give Biological Children Space

Several couples who dealt with significant behavioral issues with their adopted children commented on the value of occasional respite time without the adopted child. I realize there are varying opinions on this, but some families said this was very important for their family's emotional health; providing space for their biological children to process and work through their feelings was essential. One-on-one meetings with each parent and each child were also seen as effective, as they ensured that biological children were not losing personal connection with their parents and made room for the children to have undivided attention.

Children can't always put words to the stress they are experiencing. I observed that parents who had biological children who were quite young (infant to age five) at the time of the adoption sometimes saw their children acting out of character. It seemed that feelings of stress and chaos were at the root of their misbehavior and tantrums. It is good to be mindful of these behaviors, and some families found that counseling or play therapy, even with very young biological children, was beneficial in helping the kids process their emotions. Just because some children can't verbalize what they are experiencing doesn't mean they aren't feeling stress due to changes in the family. Toddlers are often most keen on picking up the emotions of their parents; therefore, the stress their parents experience, they experience too.

Paul and Lindsey, parents of two adopted girls and three biological children, talked at length about the stress that existed in their home with the addition of their two adopted daughters and the challenges of blending their family. They decided to pursue several family counseling sessions with just their biological children. The counselor's office proved to be a helpful environment for their kids to express how they felt, talk about the challenges, and work toward ways they could better integrate as a new family. "I've learned it's messy at times," said Lindsey, "and I have to be okay with that. I remind myself that [my adopted daughters'] past trauma is always there, and they need to be parented differently. I also tell myself that I can't make an angry, traumatized child the center of my home. God has to remain at the center."

Don't Take on the Emotions of Biological Children

"I would dread going to pick up the kids from school," admitted Shannon, mother of two adopted and two biological kids. The two children that Shannon and her husband added to their family were older than their biological children by several years. "My youngest daughter resented them so much. She would say things like, 'Mommy, do you remember when Ana and David weren't here and we would do this and that?' She wanted to let them know that she was there first. She was trying to create a separation between *us* and *them*."

Shannon also acknowledged that as she watched her biological daughters respond negatively, she had trouble separating their emotions from her own.

> I felt I was taking on some of the emotions our daughters were feeling. My husband and I have talked about this and what it would be like if we

didn't already have biological kids. I really think this would have been easier. We wouldn't have had this idea of what family was. But we did this family thing for six years and then we brought in two ten-year-olds. This was now our family, and it didn't feel natural. What were we supposed to do as parents to these kids we just met? It felt like someone said, "Here are your kids, now love them." Looking back, I think I just wanted all the kids to get along so that we would feel like a family. Then we got to a point of acceptance that it may not ever be exactly how we envision it.

Moving into a different house turned out to be a good thing for our family, as the new house contained memories of "the six of us." There were no memories in the new home of how it had been before the adoption. A lot cleared up in that move alone. We were in a new neighborhood creating new memories. Three years later, a lot of growth has taken place in our family. It was "us" and "them" for so long, and now it's not that way in our girls' eyes. They've not only become siblings; they've finally become friends.

Help Children Understand Different Parenting Approaches

One of the unforeseen challenges I continually heard about was how both biological and adopted children compared themselves to each other, particularly around the issue of discipline. Upon comparing the discipline they were receiving to the way parents treated biological kids, adopted kids often concluded that they were being punished unfairly. This was especially true if the adopted child was close in age to the children already in the home.

Lindsey explained the tension that existed in their home as they integrated two new kids into a household that already ran a certain way: "When you have your biological kids for so long, you have your set way of doing things, and that gets shaken up when you adopt. Our adopted girls had lived their whole life *hiding* from authority, and now they were learning they had to *trust* authority."

Lindsey's husband, Paul, added, "When we say something to correct our bio kids, we have sixteen years of history and care. They know and trust our love. I can get on my son's case because he has a foundation with us, so he knows I love him. Our adopted daughter instead points out that we're always disciplining her, and her brother isn't getting disciplined like she is. What she doesn't see is that he's already learned a lot of his lessons and so doesn't need to be disciplined the same way. They are close in age, so it's hard for her to see that she's being corrected more than he is."

Jayne and Roger Clark added eleven-year-old Max and his older sister to their family of five. Their biological son Peter was about the same age as Max when he came home. Roger shared that early on, Max would constantly say, "Why am I always getting in trouble and Peter never gets in trouble?" Roger went on: "I had to explain to Max that Peter got in trouble for eleven years before he got here. I told him, 'Peter learned this stuff already, you just weren't here when he was learning it.' " Though the explanation didn't solve everything, Roger said that it helped put some things in perspective for Max, and in time the discrepancy in discipline became less obvious.

I also heard about instances when the biological children in the home felt that the newly adopted children were receiving special treatment. One teen girl, Hannah, shared how her two newly adopted brothers, close to her in age, didn't get in trouble for the same things she did. Hannah was adamant that her mom didn't hold the new brothers to the same standard she was held to. Since the adoption, rules at home had become stricter. In order to keep things "fair," Hannah's mother took away privileges that Hannah previously had earned, privileges that the boys were not yet ready for. Hannah's curfew became earlier and her limits on technology more stringent. "I told my mom, 'It's not fair—I've earned your trust, and they haven't! Why do *I* have to be punished because you don't trust *them?*' " Many biological kids like Hannah had a difficult time making sense of their new positions in the family and felt they'd been displaced.

Several parents I interviewed also talked about the extra nuances and challenges of adopting kids who were close in age to the family's biological children, often referred to as "twinning." I observed again and again that twinning led to more difficulties. In many cases, it intensified the issue of sibling comparison, thus increasing stress for the whole family.

Several kids mentioned that it was hard to have adopted siblings near their age who suddenly became the "cool kids" at school because of their foreign accents and unusual backgrounds. Molly, who gained a brother close to her age, felt like she lost her identity at school when her brother arrived. Before she had been "Molly"; now she was just known as "Ruslan's sister." How could her newly adopted brother have become popular overnight? Molly admitted it was hard to watch Ruslan, who was a nuisance at home, suddenly gain attention and fame at school while she transitioned to being "his sister" and faded into the background.

Some of the adopted kids I spoke with said that suddenly acquiring siblings and figuring out new dynamics was difficult for them too. Alexander shared that the hardest part of being adopted was having siblings. "It's like suddenly they're your brothers and sisters, and yet at the same time they *really* aren't. It was hard to navigate that. In the orphanage, I had to be aggressive to take care of myself, so that came out with my new siblings, especially since we were so close in age. It took a while for things to change and for us to get along."

After hearing from several families with twinned children, I concluded that extra caution and planning is warranted when considering such an adoption arrangement. If a family still chooses to move forward in adopting children close in age to their biological children, it may be helpful to discuss this complex dynamic with families who twinned their children to find out what they learned and what they might have done differently.

Have Hard and Honest Conversations Around Personal Safety

Sadly, sexual abuse is very common in institutions, and far too many kids have experienced it at the hands of a caregiver, another child in their orphanage, or by a family member or adult in their past. Many years of working in this field have taught me that you cannot go into adoption ignoring the fact that there is a strong possibility your child has experienced some form of sexual abuse and, as a result, could act out sexually.

I interviewed four families who had to walk the very difficult road of having children in their home (biological or adopted) be sexually abused by an adopted sibling. These families now understand that they could've taken more precautions to protect their children from each other; they also recognize they were operating out of naive assumptions about possible behaviors. Walking into the world of adoption means that parents need to be willing to have hard and honest conversations with their children about personal safety and touch, and not just one time, but continually—after an adopted child comes home. Consideration should also be given to rooming situations, locks on doors, and video monitors to ensure that all children are safe and protected.

The Meyers knew that bringing a preteen and a teenage girl into their home while having kids close in age was not without risk. They shared that they had ongoing conversations with their biological kids about potential safety issues in order to ensure that they were not overlooking any potential threats. Another family, who was getting ready to adopt a ten-year-old boy, talked with their younger daughters about good and bad touch and assured them that they could always tell the parents anything. Once their brother came home, these parents also made a strict rule that the children were never allowed to play alone together in one another's bedrooms. While the parents haven't witnessed alarming behavior, they recognize they cannot be too vigilant in making sure all of their children are kept safe.

Resiliency and Growth

Clearly, adding an adopted child to the mix of an established family is not without bumps in the road. As many parents noted, watching their biological kids navigate the ups and downs of the adjustment was harder than they anticipated and impacted their own emotions deeply. Several families said that seeing their biological children struggle was one of the biggest stresses of the family integration. Yet many parents also shared how their biological children are stronger and more resilient as a result of the adoption. They have seen their kids grow in compassion and forgiveness as they've learned to share, adapt, and give sacrificially.

The Browns adopted a girl about the same age as their oldest biological daughter and also had two younger sons. In the early days of bringing their daughter home, there were many tantrums, door slams, and days of the silent treatment. There were hopeful moments with little breakthroughs sprinkled in, but the emotional rollercoaster the entire family was experiencing became exhausting. The Browns often worried about how they had wounded their biological children through the chaos they had welcomed into their home. There were many days when they especially doubted if they'd done the right thing in adopting a teen.

The mother, Amy, shared, "At one point I had to tell my other kids how sorry I was for putting them through it all and how hard it was for me to see them have to go through this pain." She paused for a moment and then, through tears, finished her thought. "Their response was amazing. They said they wouldn't change anything because of what our relationships are now. 'It's okay Mom,' they said, 'We'll be okay. We're closer now as a result of all of this.' "

Amy and her husband have come to a place where they recognize that God is using everything, their mistakes included. In spite of the difficult moments and wondering if they could have done things differently, they can now see how God has used the challenges of their adoption to develop and mold their children into healthy and loving young adults. They appreciate how their family has bonded through the challenging aspects of integrating an adopted sibling.

The Browns, like other families, have learned that becoming an integrated family unit simply takes time. Some people enter into adoption thinking that the first year or two will be hard, but after that they'll settle into a new normal. For some of the families I know, this was the case, but others commented that even four or five years later they are still struggling to be a family. They said that it's important to be gracious with yourself and your children and recognize that your family has changed forever. There is no magic timeline for feeling like a family. It may never feel the way it did before, but trust that God is working to refine you and your children through the process.

As one father stated, "Normal can become an idol, so embrace the place you are and see what God is doing." His wife Lindsey added, "Looking back, I'd tell myself that just like Moses sought to enter the promised land but never made it in his lifetime, I need to be committed to the mission and not to the success of the mission. Battles can be sanctification."

For Reflection or Group Discussion

1. If you have both biological and adopted children, what effect did the adoption and their new relationships have on them?

2. If you have adopted, have your biological children freely expressed emotions about the adoption (positive or negative)? Describe what they've shared.

3. If you have both biological and adopted children, in what ways have your adopted children compared themselves to your biological children?

4. Prior to adoption, did you think about the effects of changing birth order? If so, how have your views changed, or have they stayed the same?

Road Rage

Spiritual Warfare and Adoption

For the cause of the orphan we fight a very real battle against a very real Enemy—an adversary who is unequivocally committed to "steal, kill and destroy" that which God created to be good (John 10:10), including families. We stand for what God stands for, the hopeless and helpless, and stand against what He opposes, the Enemy establishing a destructive foothold in the lives of families and children. It is a spiritual battle at its core.[1]

—JASON JOHNSON, WRITER AND SPEAKER

I t was late August, and we were putting on a camp in southern Ukraine for a group of orphaned teens who'd either just graduated the orphanage or were nearing the end of their studies. A group of us were hanging out on the beach, enjoying the warm rays of the late afternoon sun, when I noticed one of the girls pulling a jellyfish out of the water and placing it on the sand.

"What are you doing?" I asked. "It will die if it isn't in the water."

"It's just one jellyfish," she said with a laugh. "It doesn't really matter."

She proceeded to pull more jellyfish out of the sea, depriving them of oxygen, and left them on the beach.

I felt anger and sadness as I watched the slow jellyfish deaths. Not that I'm overly sympathetic to jellyfish (I really don't like them), but the fact that this teenager was intentionally pulling them onto the beach to die struck a nerve in me.

As I pondered what was taking place, I remembered a contrasting story often told in adoption circles about a beach strewn with starfish. In the story, a young man encounters the stranded creatures and is overcome with the desire to rescue them, so he bends down and begins to throw the starfish back into the ocean, one by one. A naysayer looking on questions what he's doing, and the young man replies, "The sun is up and the tide is going out. If I don't throw them in, they'll die."

The naysayer responds, "But young man, don't you realize that there are miles and miles of beach and starfish all along it? You can't possibly make a difference!"

The young man listens politely, then bends down, picks up another starfish, and throws it into the sea. He turns to the onlooker and declares, "It made a difference for that one!"[2]

This story has inspired many people to pursue adoption or to perform other acts of selfless service. It's a story I've replayed in my mind when negative thoughts have crept in and whispered that my efforts aren't having much of an impact. The story helps me remember that it's always about the "one"—stopping for one child, ministering to one child, seeing one child gain a family.

The starfish parable together with this new jellyfish spin struck me as profoundly ironic. I was watching the reversal of the beloved tale at the hands of an orphaned girl. It all seemed so wrong. As this young teen pulled each jellyfish out of the water, I felt as though God was giving me a concrete picture of the spiritual warfare surrounding adoption—a fight for the orphan and every vulnerable child.

The work of placing children in families isn't just about throwing starfish back into the ocean so they can live—it's making sure we're overcoming the work of an enemy who is fighting desperately to leave children struggling for breath, out of the life-giving water. As busy as we are throwing starfish into the sea to find life, an enemy is at work trying to pull them right back out.

Steve Weber, the former regional director of the Christian Broadcasting Network in Ukraine and the family member I worked alongside in ministry, is often quoted in the global orphan care world as saying, "Adoption is not charity; it's spiritual warfare." An adoptive father himself, Steve is aware that when we enter the arena of adoption and orphan care, we enter into a spiritual battle. In the introduction of his book *The Screwtape Letters*, C. S. Lewis wrote, "There are two equal and opposite errors into which our race can fall about the devils. One is to disbelieve in their existence. The other is to believe, and to feel an excessive and unhealthy interest in them. They themselves are equally pleased by both errors."[3] It's with this guiding thought that I tackle the topic of spiritual warfare.

In the Heat of the Battle

In the Western world, we tend to pay little attention to opposing forces in the spiritual realm. In contrast, in countries throughout Africa, Latin America, and Asia, people understand that there are powers of good and evil fighting against one another, not only among those who hold Christian beliefs but among people from various belief systems. They don't take the truth of good and evil lightly.

Over the years, I've met and interacted with people who seem to have a heightened awareness of spiritual atmospheres. Whether in a building, a city, or a nation, some seem more attuned to what is happening in the invisible realm and can sense darkness—or peace—in a place.

Several families I spoke with described certain times of interacting with their children when they felt an unsettling presence in their home, typically soon after adopting. One family admitted it felt strange to talk about the topic openly, but as they shared their experience with others, they realized they were not alone in feeling like something invisible but intense was going on at a spiritual level.

I want to be clear that I do not in any way mean that every behavior, neurological issue, or struggle a child faces is a spiritual or demonic attack. We need to view children holistically and not look for a demon under every rock. That said, we should not downplay the spiritual aspect of what may be happening and ignore how it can wreak havoc in a home. We need to give consideration and weight to what might be going on spiritually in the life of each child so that we can do battle with evil effectively. "For we do not wrestle against flesh and blood, but against the rulers, against the authorities, against the cosmic powers of this present darkness, against the spiritual forces of evil in the heavenly places." (Ephesians 6:10–12 ESV).

The longer I've worked with children in institutions and seen some of the evil perpetrated against vulnerable children, the more I've seen the need to break spiritual strongholds. It is one thing for a family to encounter spiritual darkness and oppression in an orphanage and something else to realize that they're dealing with the same darkness and oppression in their home.

There's a war against children in this world, and even more so against unprotected, parentless children. Whether it be through violence, neglect, or abandonment, an enemy tries to keep children from knowing God, and that enemy is also set on keeping them from fulfilling their God-given purpose. The Devil does not want to see children in families; he wants them in institutions, where they are outside of the parental protection the family provides and more vulnerable to his influences.

Years ago I attended a ministry school in England that provided teaching on what it means to have a spiritual covering. When we're born, God gives us parents to be like a spiritual umbrella. Parents filter what and who their children have access to—and what and who has access to them. If parents are fulfilling their God-given responsibility, then they are doing their best to keep their children safe. As I listened to the lectures and gave more thought to this spiritual covering, my mind drifted to the children I knew in Ukrainian orphanages. Children deprived of parental care have lost that spiritual covering, and as a result, the Devil uses every opportunity to oppress and destroy them when they are most exposed.

In my early days of bringing programs into orphanages, I quickly realized that television was usually the group's primary babysitter. Children who spent time in a Ukrainian institution likely had an extensive diet of horror films and graphic sexual content presented in the common living area. There were times when I stood by in shock as I realized how much freedom kids were given to view shows that I was uncomfortable watching. Along with the TV babysitter came the introduction of the smartphone. Many kids and teens in institutions now have access to phones and unsupervised internet streaming, with danger only a click away.

During summer camps our ministry provided, or prior to taking children to the US for a summer hosting trip, I would survey kids about their various likes, including their favorite kinds of movies. Nine times out of ten the answer would be "horror movies." I was grieved when I learned that not only was this what they were exposed to daily, it was also what they wanted to continue watching. I think of the children who have struggled with chronic night terrors or those who have severe pornography addictions and am keenly aware that the enemy used their vulnerabilities while they were living outside of parental covering.

Even when children are adopted, the enemy wants them to keep seeing themselves as parentless. I've heard it said repeatedly that it's one thing to take a child out of an orphanage but another thing altogether to take the orphanage out of the child. The enemy delights in preventing children from gaining childlike trust and finding healing from past wounds. For it is in healing and trust that children can learn to discard their orphan spirit and become a true son or daughter, ideally to both their adoptive parents and to God.

Russell Moore, adoptive father and president of the Ethics & Religious Liberty Commission of the Southern Baptist Convention, writes and speaks extensively on the topic of adoption and often comments on how spiritual warfare is common in the adoption arena. He says that when he speaks to prospective families about adopting children, spiritual warfare is one of the first things he brings up, which surprises some families.

> Throughout the Bible, you see the forces of this world consistently coming into conflict with children—Pharaoh in Egypt with the Israelite children, Herod with the children in Bethlehem. Why?

I think it's because the devil knows that what Jesus said is true, that those who come into the kingdom of God come as little children. There's a visible image of newness of life, of dependence and vulnerability that Jesus has called us to, of related-ness, and continuity of generations. Children are always, in every context, going to be warred against. . . .

. . . So, when you have a family who is moving toward caring for the vulnerable through adoption, foster care, or orphan care of any kind, they're going to be troubling some things that don't want to be troubled.

You need more than just good preparation for parenting, more than a good support system, more than a safe home. You also need prayer, a church home, and an ongoing sense of the Spirit in walking forward in whatever it is that God has given you with adoption or orphan care.[4]

The Power of Prayer

Many of the families I interviewed had little to no teaching or experience concerning spiritual warfare or demonic oppression prior to adoption. However, many discovered spiritual strongholds when they brought children into their homes and began taking steps to establish a spiritual umbrella over their families. Only through increasing their understanding of this topic did they learn ways to battle oppression successfully.

Several families I interviewed noted how prayer was particularly effective in bringing about change. When they encountered a sense of darkness in their home, they learned about the power of prayer in a whole new way. By praying in the name of Jesus, specifically, they saw a distinct change in their child or the atmosphere of their home.

"I sensed that Satan didn't want good for our boys and doesn't want them to thrive in a family," shared Lucy, an adoptive mom of two teenage sons. "I sensed that I needed to claim Jesus and pray against evil—even to name it for them, to name the lies the enemy was feeding the boys so that they could see what they were up against."

Cara, who came from a faith tradition that provided little teaching on spiritual warfare, shared about feeling a dark spiritual presence in their home after adopting their son Sam.

> Odd things started happening once we brought him home from Ukraine. I had this picture that I bought from a church there, and I hung it on the wall and it would just fall down from the wall all the time. I also had this huge window ledge in my kitchen, and I had a picture of each of the children there. The picture of Sam would periodically fall off the ledge. I'd be working in front of the sink, and all of sudden his picture would just fall, right in front of my eyes. I never got scared; I just

realized I needed to be praying against something demonic right then.

Things started getting really bad with Sam right around that time. We brought him home in August, and I felt like things came to a crescendo by April. When I went to an appointment with my chiropractor, who was a Christian, I asked him to pray for us as things were really hard. He's one of those people who prays for you and you feel it. He said to me, "Cara, I just feel like the Lord wants me to tell you that what you're battling against is not this boy but something dark around this boy." Then a few days later a man who is a former orphan came to visit us and said, "I'm thirty-eight and I *still* see monsters. You have to recognize that there are demons that harass him." He gave us some anointing oil and told us to anoint the rooms in our house and to pray. I thought, "That's not us, that's not our faith history, we're not Holy Rollers." But we did it; we anointed Sam and anointed door frames and Sam's room and his closet, and it helped. As time passed, if I would see a picture drop I would automatically think, "We need to pray," and over time it all stopped.

I don't share such stories to present a formula for battling evil but instead to highlight families' experiences with encountering spiritual darkness in their homes and seeing it lift through the power of prayer. This goes for the children as well. Numerous families referenced placing scripture in visible places for their child to see, praying scripture over their child (with permission), and teaching their child the power of praying in Jesus' name.

Heather, who adopted her daughters when they were six and eight, shared that shortly after bringing the girls home she felt things that were not normal in the house. "Some of the tantrums that took place brought about a demonic darkness in our home. It became clear that it wasn't just the girls' behavior we were fighting against. One night, one of our girls started rocking uncontrollably for a long period of time and began pulling out her hair. As we started praying for her, we saw a breakthrough. There was one night in particular that she recognized that prayer was what helped her the most. She kept saying, 'Papa, when you pray, I no cry.'"

Sue and Laurence Peterson faced a major battle when they adopted Yana right after she turned sixteen. They admit there was no honeymoon period with their daughter, and from the moment she entered their home they felt some sort of spiritual oppression. The Peterson family's story is notedly one of the most extreme stories I heard on this topic, and I wasn't sure if I would include it in my writing. However, to me, their honest, firsthand experience underscores the reality of the demonic realm and the power it can have when it finds a door to enter.

"We experienced stuff like you see in movies," shared Laurence. "About three different times, we felt there was strong demonic activity in our house. The worst night, it was a three-hour episode. It was like another presence took over Yana's body. She had tried to lock herself in the bathroom and I put my arm in the door to keep her from locking it. As I opened the door, she turned and caught a glimpse of herself in the mirror and seemed almost frightened. 'That's not me,' she cried. 'No, Yana, that's not you,' I said. 'That's why you need to call on the name of Jesus, and He will help you.' "

About a year after bringing their daughter home, the Petersons temporarily took in Larisa, another adopted Ukrainian girl from their community who had been going through some difficulties with her family.

> One evening, we couldn't calm Larisa down. She was seeing things coming after her, and it felt like this demonic attack, and we prayed for over an hour. Yana was having an episode at the *exact* same time. Finally, Yana said, "Help me, Jesus." We encouraged her to keep saying it, but she told us, "They won't let me, they'll kill me." It took forever to get her to say it again, but when she finally repeated, "Help me, Jesus," everything stopped, just like that. This happened on two different occasions. When she said, "Help me, Jesus," it was like the temperature in the room changed, like she woke up from a dream.
>
> When it happened again, I asked, "Do you have anything in your possession that is opening this house to the Devil?" She admitted that night that

our two girls and another adopted girl had had some séances upstairs. They had gotten a spell book at a used bookstore and were apparently doing something weird and demonic, taking oaths and who knows what else. They had a poem from a song that was demonic and other things related to witchcraft, and we cleaned it all out and explained the danger. At that point, a lot of things changed for the better.

Clearly these teenage girls were dabbling in the occult, which the Petersons believed opened a door for a heightened level of demonic activity. They were holistic in their approach with Yana and had their daughter psychologically tested for possible mental health issues, but doctors didn't give them any diagnosis other than the effects of her traumatic childhood.

To me, the experiences these families had serve as a reminder that there truly is a world we do not see, and we need to be prepared and remember to fight our battle with the powerful weapons of prayer and the Word of God. As Paul wrote in his second letter to the Corinthians, "For though we walk in the flesh, we are not waging war according to the flesh. For the weapons of our warfare are not of the flesh but have divine power to destroy strongholds" (2 Corinthians 10:3–4 ESV).

Winning the Battle

What amazed me most as parents shared their stories around the topic of spiritual warfare is that, ultimately, these were not stories of fear or discouragement. Rather, they were experiences that awakened parents to the importance of their role and caused them to conclude that, if the enemy was attacking, they were headed in the right direction.

Lindsey, an adoptive mother of two, shared candidly about her experiences with what she considered to be spiritual warfare around the time leading up to the adoption.

> I've never struggled with more spiritual warfare than when we were adopting. It's uncanny some of the things we've gone through. The minute we decided we were going to adopt our daughter, literally everything went wrong. Our finances were a mess, our roof fell apart, our well went dry, our insurance premiums went up, we had two frozen water pipes—all within fourteen months! I said, "I can't do this, everything is going wrong!" We didn't have great support, and I kept thinking, "How are we going to get through this?" But it was in these times that we learned to depend on the Lord more than ever, and we've all learned more about His character and provision through everything we've been through.

Gail and Gary Henderson have four Ukrainian teens in their home, three of whom are biological siblings. They said that they cannot imagine how their children could have found any deep healing or freedom apart from what Jesus has done supernaturally in their lives. "Unless you're in prayer every day about your kids, they're never going to be truly healed," Gail said. "I believe Christ is the only One who can completely fill them. . . . The depth of loss and pain that kids from a trauma background go through is never going to be fixed by us as parents, or anyone else that comes into their lives. There are some elements of healing that only the Lord can do. I see before my eyes the aspects where Jesus is transforming my kids and healing them. With my two kids who have accepted Christ and are pursuing Him, I see the most transformation and change."

Other parents I spoke with expressed the need they've recognized for deeper spiritual transformation in themselves. One father said,

> I don't think we fully understood the impact of where our girls came from. They were orphaned because of the work of the enemy. God doesn't will that kids be raised away from their biological parents, so any scenario that makes a kid a social orphan is demonic. There is darkness that created the world they lived in, and they had to learn to just survive. When we took all that darkness and brought it into our house, I wasn't expecting it to expose the darkness in me. I'd been around a lot of kids, but I'd never been provoked in this way

before adopting. Usually I'm cool under fire; I don't overreact. But suddenly I found myself asking, "Where did these dark emotions come from?" I came to realize that my deficiencies were exploited by theirs.

Now, seven years later, we still face day-one battles at times. We're not there yet. Every day is a clear reminder that we are fighting to be family. It's reassuring to know that Jesus isn't finished with our stories. I believe He will win this battle for us.

For Reflection or Group Discussion

1. Have you ever experienced spiritual warfare? If you have adopted, did you experience spiritual warfare while preparing to adopt your child?

2. If you have adopted, was spiritual warfare something you discussed prior to your adoption?

3. If you have adopted, once you brought your child home, were there specific times that you felt you were fighting a spiritual battle? Please describe.

4. If you have adopted, did your prayer life change after adoption? If so, how?

8

Detours and Road Closures

Stories of Adoption Disruption

People were mystified. We had this community that supported us in the adoption, and then they were left confused. They'd not fully understood what we were doing to begin with, and then they watched as it all fell apart.

—ADOPTIVE MOTHER

While families navigate their way through the varying challenges that adoption brings, there are times when some have needed to make the painful decision to find a new home or living option for their adopted child. This is known as adoption disruption, or sometimes "rehoming," and it is a concept that remains saturated with controversy.

Disrupted adoption gained much public attention in 2010, when an American mother put her then seven-year-old adopted son from Russia on a one-way flight to Moscow by himself. The story quickly made international headlines, and the mother was harshly criticized and villainized. The topic of "failed" adoptions suddenly gained traction as people began asking the question, "What could possibly have gone so wrong that someone would send their kid back?"

Though I would never advocate for sending a child alone on an airplane back to a country of origin, I recognize there was something much deeper going on in the story of that mother and son. In my early days of being involved in the adoption world, I may have been the critical bystander to any family who had seemingly "given up on a child." But after sitting with numerous families and hearing and sometimes watching their stories unfold, I've learned to listen first and then ask questions before jumping to any conclusions about what a family should have done. If we haven't walked a mile in someone else's shoes, we never know the full story. As with many things surrounding adoption, I'm learning not to draw hard and fast lines when it comes to disruption.

For some people, the concept of disruption is very black and white. I've talked to several families that use the logic of never disrupting an adoption for the same reason they'd never consider a divorce: it is a lifelong commitment and covenant. Though I appreciate the sentiments of this argument and believe some parallels can be drawn, I also think it's a faulty analogy—one that has led to harsh judgment of those facing the very difficult decision as to whether or not a child should remain in their home. No two stories are the same. Sometimes I've questioned if a particular disruption was necessary or if the family had truly exhausted all options, but I've also seen it become overwhelmingly clear that finding a new family for an adopted child was in the best interests of both the child and the family. Always, the decision was made as a last resort.

Unheard Stories

On my journey across the US, I sat with six different families who experienced the anguish of deciding to place their child(ren) in another home. There were an additional seven families who sent their children to boarding schools or therapeutic treatment centers, or whose teen children made the decision to leave the family and find their own way. Among the families I spoke to, 16 kids out of the 141 represented, experienced some form of disruption. The families I spoke with allowed me to ask hard questions as they unpacked their stories about what led them to disrupt their adoptions. For each of these families, adoption disruption was one of the most heartbreaking and lonely experiences they'd been through and one they'd never imagined would happen.

Initially, I was hesitant to ask these families if they'd be open to sharing their experiences with me for my research. After all, the last time I'd sat with them was when their glasses were still rosy, and the word *disruption* hadn't yet entered their vocabulary, let alone their minds. I wondered if they'd be willing to dig up memories that were surely quite excruciating. Would they be ready to share their stories, or was it too soon? I was amazed when all of the families I contacted responded with a yes. Many said they felt their stories were overlooked and unheard in the adoption world. They wanted to share more so that prospective families might learn from their experiences, and even their mistakes, and be able to approach a potential adoption with eyes a bit more open than theirs had been.

As I entered into each of these families' homes, I understood I was treading on tender hearts still in the process of making sense of the way their stories had unfolded. For this reason, I am humbled that they chose to share their journeys so vulnerably.

The Harding Family

I still remember the phone call I got one winter evening from the Hardings, a family I'd met briefly through some other adoptive parents. They had three biological children and had come to Ukraine to adopt a daughter. After hosting ten-year-old Diana, who was close in age to their middle son, the Hardings moved forward with her adoption. As they were wrapping up paperwork and saying their goodbyes at the orphanage, one of Diana's older friends, Marina, approached them and asked if they would take her as well. Marina was fifteen and about to age out of the orphanage. The Hardings had grown to care for Marina while visiting Diana each day, and she seemed to be like a big sister or surrogate mother to Diana. When Marina approached them about adopting her, they were moved with compassion, thinking that perhaps they could update their documents and come back to adopt Marina before she had to leave the orphanage in a few months.

As the Hardings recounted the story to me on the phone and asked for my opinion, I hesitantly shared that in my experience, coming back to adopt unrelated kids from the same orphanage hadn't always proved to be a good thing. I'd observed that sometimes adopting two unrelated children could make it difficult for both of them to find healing in the same home. Despite adding my two cents, I knew that this family ultimately had to pray, seek God's will, and make their own decision about how to proceed.

Four months later, they were back in my apartment in Kyiv pursuing Marina's adoption. Four years after that, I was sitting in *their* living room, hearing their account of making the very painful decision to find another home for Marina in the United States.

I asked David, the father, to share what he remembered about those days when they were first considering adopting Marina. "We liked Marina, we cared about her," he said. "She was a friend to Diana and the girls seemed so sad to part. I felt like we suddenly had the power not to separate them. We'd heard stories from the hosting agencies that [about] 90 percent of these girls end up in prostitution, and when you're there you feel like you have the ability to stop that from happening. It seemed simple: we could rescue another girl. We prayed about it and thought it was the right thing to do. . . . But looking back, I'll say we were fundamentally underinformed about the complexity of

(a) adoption and (b) adopting two different kids with differing trauma."

Within just a week of trying to juggle five children and helping Marina adjust to their family and learn the language, things began to spiral into chaos. Diana, who prior to Marina's arrival had been adjusting well, suddenly began to pull away, and the behaviors of both girls became very concerning for their parents.

"We didn't understand what we had done in adopting two kids from the same orphanage with these enmeshed backgrounds," David said. "Marina encouraged Diana to pull away from us immediately and got her to speak only Russian again, whereas before Marina came, Diana had been making so much progress with learning English. Right away we saw that Diana stopped bonding with us and her siblings and would only go to Marina. Then Marina started to tell our youngest son she would harm him. It seemed that she saw tormenting our youngest son as a way to get to us. As things got worse, she also demanded that we send her back to Ukraine."

As months passed, the Hardings sought help wherever they could. Marina's behavior was escalating as she tried to control the situation around her, and she would regularly fly into fits of rage. Diana withdrew from the family more and more. It seemed the Hardings were losing not just one but two children.

Sharon, the mom, shared how hard it was to watch all of this unfold before their eyes. "I think that when we first brought Diana home, she enjoyed the new start, but when we brought Marina here, we brought the orphanage back to Diana, and she didn't know how to cope. One day she just completely cratered. She eventually stopped speaking altogether, and she began harming herself as well."

The Hardings were watching their relationships with both girls disintegrate in front of their eyes and were also seeing their biological boys retreat from the family. They were desperate to find help for their daughters and a solution that would get them through this difficult period. "We kept trying to lean in and make it work," David shared. "We continued talking to different counselors and everyone kept saying, 'You need to get these girls apart.' One therapist we greatly respect and who has a lot of experience working with adopted and traumatized kids told us the girls were 'unhealthily enmeshed' and he didn't think they could heal in our home if they remained together. So to get a break, we did a short respite and sent Marina to be with some of our friends for a few days. Immediately Diana's disposition changed, and she relaxed. At that point we looked into residential programs for Marina because we could see that we needed to get them apart. But no doors seemed to be opening."

As the Hardings started to understand that bringing healing to both daughters under one roof wasn't possible, the words "adoption disruption" entered their vocabulary for the first time. They shared that it was one of the most difficult seasons of their lives. "I was very much in a dark hole," Sharon said. "How did I mishear God? What had I done wrong?"

A second respite family came forward for Marina, and in time this same family felt they could provide the healing home she needed. They were an older couple with no children remaining at home, and it seemed this was the kind of environment that could help Marina. The couple offered to adopt her. The Hardings were reeling after all that had happened but were amazed at the way God provided another family for their older daughter.

Shortly after Marina went to live with the other family, Sharon was still struggling with understanding why all these things had happened the way they did. She shared with me about a call she had with Marina's new family after a few months had passed.

> I was really struggling, but a huge blessing for me was when we had a Skype call with the family that was in the process of adopting Marina. As we spoke, the mom teared up and said, "I don't think I would've ever gone to Ukraine to get Marina, but I think God sent you there to bring her to us. I know it's been very hard on your family, and we're sorry about that—but we're really thankful for her, and we feel like God worked through your family to bring her into our family." That comment meant a lot to me. It helped give me new perspective. Marina needed a lot of attention and one-on-one time, and this couple could provide what was best.

It was difficult for the Hardings to share all they had experienced with friends and family. How do you explain disrupting an adoption so soon after bringing a child home? Sharon conveyed that initially they felt judged by some in their community who didn't fully understand what was happening. "People were mystified because we had this community that supported us in the adoption, and then they were left confused. They hadn't fully understood what we were doing to begin with, and then they watched as it all fell apart. It was hard to know what to share. We tried very hard not to talk badly about Marina. We didn't blame her. We knew she was a hurting kid in a new culture, and in many ways we failed her just as much as she failed to integrate into our family."

The Hardings' story is a difficult one. They were parents who desperately wanted to see both of the girls in their home find healing, and it took great humility and courage to recognize that what they initially thought was best for everyone was not going to be the solution for either girl.

I will not belittle the trauma that a girl like Marina has gone through by being brought to a foreign country and then readopted into another home. However, I also believe that keeping a child in a family where healing cannot happen is not in anyone's best interest. In this situation, the Hardings were able to identify that Marina would do better in a family without children, and ultimately, that proved to be the place where she could be given a second chance.

The Tayler Family

The Taylers also made the very difficult decision to disrupt their adoption. Nick and Sarah Tayler had eight biological children when they felt the desire to add to their family through adoption. After researching many options, they committed to pursuing two Ukrainian girls with special needs through an organization that was advocating for the girls. They had pictures of these soon-to-be daughters displayed in their home and fundraised fiercely to get to Ukraine.

Just days before they were ready to travel, the Taylers received the devastating news that one of these daughters had passed away. They were in shock and heartbroken. But with the knowledge that the other little girl was left waiting, they flew to Ukraine as scheduled.

I remember meeting with Nick and Sarah in my apartment and their tender hearts as they shared about the loss of the little girl they'd hoped to bring home. The next day, their appointment at the state adoption department provided more devastating news. There had been a mistake in the paperwork. The other girl they'd come for was not registered and therefore not available for adoption.

The Taylers were left reeling. What should they do now? The advocating organization placed before them binders full of other children waiting for families. Yet they were still grieving and in complete shock over losing the two girls they'd been praying for and had assumed would be their daughters.

"Looking back, we should have walked out of that room," Sarah said. "But there was the social pressure of all these people who were watching. I wish we'd had an exit plan. We should have waited at least twenty-four hours before we made any decisions. But there we were, and there was the pressure to pick another child. We kept thinking about all the people who'd donated money so we could adopt, and now there were other kids in front of us who all needed homes." The Taylers walked out of the appointment with the files of two new children—unrelated kids at the same orphanage. The boy, Mark, was two, and the girl, Daria, was nine.

Nick had been researching the statistics surrounding orphans being trafficked and admits now that he felt like he was on a mission to rescue a little girl from a potentially horrendous future. Sarah can now look back and see that, throughout the entire process, she was out of her comfort zone but kept following her husband's lead, praying that her emotions would get in line. In spite of Sarah's reservations, the Taylers kept pressing forward on a rescue mission. Within a couple of months, they were home with their two new children and faced with integrating them into their well-established culture and rhythm of eight other children. Sarah shared:

> We thought we would just be able to absorb additional kids into our family unit. We didn't grasp the depth of it from day one. We'd gone to Ukraine for two special-needs children who were going to be the babies in our family, and that was what we'd

mentally prepared for. Suddenly we added a two-year-old toddler and a nine-year-old daughter. Daria became the middle child in the mix of seven other daughters, and I think she was literally lost and overwhelmed, and so were they. Daria was trying to figure out how to survive in our house and latched on to our youngest daughter and started pulling her away from the others. She was always trying to isolate our youngest, and as she did this, our little one started rejecting me. It was so hard to watch. I would lie in bed at night and beg for my family back. They were all here, but *every* relationship had changed, and I was devastated.

The Taylers felt helpless as they watched their tightly knit family unit cave in around them. Their children were trying to cope with what was going on in their own way, and all were struggling. Seeing their kids spiraling downward, they knew something needed to change.

The parents brought in attachment therapists to help the family make sense of things. Sarah said, "The therapist had all the kids draw a picture of our home. Daria drew a picture of the house and her picture looked like our house, but it was underwater. Suddenly, I realized that was how she felt, and that's what it looked like to watch her. It was as if she was saying, 'I'm trying, but I'm lost in this place.' "

The Taylers were advised that Daria would likely do best in a home where she was the youngest child. They were also told that it might be only a matter of time before she abused the youngest child in the home. That was the final information the Taylers needed. "We realized we'd hit a place where we were no longer able to help anyone, and that was very scary," Sarah said. "Sometimes I think we could've done it if it was just Nick and her and me; but sadly, you can't take a little girl with some serious issues and plop her in the middle of healthy people and expect her to get healthy. Everyone else was getting sick instead, and we didn't know how to make anyone better. What breaks my heart is that none of this was her fault, and yet she bore the consequences."

Nick added, "We picked a kid out of a book, in a crisis moment. How were we to know if she could make it in our family? It's a flawed system, how they have you pick children. I don't think we realized how tight of a family we were and that perhaps we weren't suited to bring an older child into the middle of that."

Ultimately, the Taylers made the heart-wrenching decision to place both children in new homes. Though there were no concerning behavioral issues with two-year-old Mark, they recognized that their family was in such a state of disrepair that they lacked the ability to parent him in the way he needed. In order for him to thrive and for their family to heal, Mark needed to be in a family that could focus on him and foster healthy attachment with him.

Within six months of the Taylers bringing the children home, both had been placed in new adoptive families, and the Taylers were left grieving and devastated as they faced the fact that they weren't able to follow through on what they'd promised. In the midst of their distress, however, they also recognized that they'd made the decision to let both children go to different families with the best interests of all in mind.

An outsider looking in on this story might find it easy to say that the family should have never come home with kids to begin with, as they were still in the throes of grieving the loss of the two little girls they'd come for. They shouldn't have been forced to pick other children without more than a moment to catch their breath. But the reality is, their story highlights the failings of an adoption system that allows prospective parents to flip open a book and pick a child knowing very little about the child's history or needs. The Taylers were pressured by a facilitation team to "rescue a child," so that's what they did. But they weren't prepared to parent a child with needs like Daria's. I think it was braver for them to recognize that they needed to make the best decision for all involved, and to do so quickly, rather than continuing to struggle to find ways to make it work.

My heart still breaks for Daria. The Taylers' hearts still break for Daria. As Sarah said through tears, "I will always have a Daria-sized hole in my heart. I'm sorry we failed her." Daria was a young girl simply trying to survive the best way she knew how, but an adoption that was meant to be healing turned toxic—toxic for the biological kids and, without her fully comprehending it, toxic for Daria, too, as she treaded water to stay afloat, all the while drowning in the house she'd drawn underwater.

Sarah shared how they feared the community would judge them, and although there were a lot of negative reactions from the online adoption community, they also received grace and support from those who knew them best.

> I had one woman come up to me and say, "We know the kind of people you are, and this must have been really, really hard. In many ways I think it was perhaps more honorable to get these kids the help they needed if you recognized you couldn't do it yourself." Her comment and her kindness meant so much to me. I was talking recently to a woman who has helped place children in new homes after disruptions and she said that in her observations, the second placement often works really well because the first family has figured out what the kids need. . . . In some ways, I feel like we were the family that kept them for a short time in order to determine what their needs were and then help identify the type of family where they would best thrive.

Other Reasons for Disruption

One family I spoke with went through the agony of having several of their young children sexually molested by the child they adopted. Sadly, this little girl had undergone repeated sexual abuse at the hands of her own biological brother (both pre- and post-adoption), and she knew no other way to connect than to act out sexually. Currently, she remains in permanent residential care, and even the facility where she resides says for her own safety and the safety of others, she should never go back into a home where other children are present. The brother was prosecuted for his abuse of his sister and is currently serving a prison sentence. The family admitted that they were completely unaware of the fact that the risk of sexual abuse in Ukrainian institutions is high. They also realized that in their large family, they didn't have the precautions set up to protect such an incident from happening, as they simply lacked the knowledge of what to look for and didn't see the warning signs that were likely present.

Another family disrupted their adoption because the extreme and chronic abuse their daughter experienced in her early childhood (which they were unaware of at the time of adoption) caused her to continually rage and prevented her from adapting to family life. As they observed their other children bearing the consequences and as the parents' own mental health began to suffer, they recognized an alternative solution was necessary. Professional therapists helped them determine that this child needed residential intervention outside the home. The family later went on to make the difficult decision of relinquishing their parental rights so that the state could provide her with the ongoing care and resources she needed.

Two other families had experiences with teen daughters who refused professional help and, after significant conflict at home, ultimately made their own decisions to leave their adoptive homes. In both situations the teens returned to Ukraine and made attempts to reconnect with biological relatives. The adoptive families were devastated that they were unable to help these girls find healing in their homes.

Adopting Teens

If you go online and start researching adoption disruption, you'll find many difficult stories and also see that the reasons behind the disruptions vary. The stories often reference children who were adopted at older ages. Some narratives scream loudly that no one should ever adopt teens and that adoption ruins lives. Other parents admit that they were simply unprepared to handle the extreme needs or behaviors of the teenage children in their care and recognized that a different family would be in the best interest of the child.

I hesitate to draw hard and fast lines on the topic of international older children and teen adoptions. I've come to recognize that, in the realm of adoption, the deeper I dig, the more I discover the subjectivity of each story and situation.

There's no doubt in my mind that adopting teens from another country (in my experience, Ukraine) is difficult and, contrary to what many might advocate, not always in the best interest of the teen. I'm personally aware of several situations where teens had doubts about wanting to be adopted and yet were talked into it by the orphanage director or facilitation team, being told it was their "only chance out." Meanwhile, the adoptive parents were unaware of that element of coercion taking place.

On my road trip, I observed very challenging situations, including "rescued" teenagers who were now single moms and a few young men who'd had multiple run-ins with the law. This has reminded me that environment alone can't change anyone. No one can go into adoption thinking that merely taking a child out of an orphanage will fix the situation.

As I reference these disruptions and other challenging situations, I also want to underscore the fact that there are many positive stories of teen adoptions. Though the transition is not easy, I have seen adolescents overcome immense challenges to integrate into a new family and a foreign culture. Some of the older kids I was able to advocate for have transitioned well overall and are even thriving in their new environment and culture. Several are now young adults who are happily married and successfully parenting (hallelujah!). In these instances, I am so thankful their parents were willing to take the risk of adopting older children, and I'm glad hard and fast lines weren't drawn that prevented these children from being adopted.

Making Sense of the Story

Adoption is often advertised as giving a child a "forever family." It's hard, therefore, to make sense of the situations where forever was not the reality. When I began this project, I was hesitant about including a chapter on disruption or at what point in the book it should be addressed. How could I frame it in a way that would be palatable and wouldn't scare all potential families away from adopting? Disruptions are confusing and hard to talk about, especially in the Christian community where we want to see a redemptive story play out. We tend to shy away from the messy areas of our lives that are still unfolding if we haven't yet turned them into a polished "testimony." We have a hard time hearing and digesting stories that don't turn out the way we think they should. But in listening to stories of disruption, we are taking into consideration the whole spectrum of adoption and gaining valuable information from families who've walked a difficult road and are still standing. I am thankful for the brave families who opened up to me and vulnerably shared their stories—ones that didn't resolve the way they hoped and prayed.

For Reflection or Group Discussion

1. Are you familiar with any disruption stories in adoption? What are your reactions to hearing about stories of adoption disruption?

2. If you have adopted, has the word "disruption" ever entered your vocabulary in regard to your own adoption? Please explain.

3. What is a way you can reach out to a family that has adopted to offer encouragement or support? If you know of a disrupted adoption, how can you encourage and support that family?

4. What spiritual and practical lessons can you learn from this chapter?

Road Repairs

On the Path toward Healing

The world breaks every one and afterward many are strong at the broken places.

—ERNEST HEMMINGWAY

One of my cousins, who was adopted at the age of two, was found the day after he was born on the streets of a city in southern Ukraine. He was wrapped in a sheet and rescued by a police officer who took him to a baby hospital. He spent the first two years of his life there, and those years were anything but healthy.

The dictionary defines healing as the process of making or becoming sound or healthy again.[1] When we think of being sick, whether dealing with physical ailments or mental anguish, we have a reference point of what we felt like before we got sick, and we long to return to that state of health. But many adopted children *never* knew health from the moment they were conceived or entered the world, so they have no point of reference to aim for.

Herein lies the challenge of helping children from hard places to find healing. How do we return to something that, in many cases, was never there to begin with? How does a child understand what health is? Keeping in mind a particular child's history of neglect, abuse, or abandonment, what is the best way to pursue healing and wholeness? The families I interviewed had as many ideas as there are children. Here are some of those ideas.

Help Children Understand Their Identity

For a large number of adopted children, knowledge of living biological parents can add a layer of difficulty when it comes to building attachments and making sense of their identity. For some of these children, memories of parents might be painful, if parental rights were revoked due to substance abuse, physical abuse, or neglect. Others remember what a parent was like and idealize that parent. For instance, a child whose parent was once sober might long for "what could have been" if things at home had turned out differently. I observed that kids who were true orphans (had no known living parents in Ukraine) often attached or adapted to their adoptive families at a faster rate than those who had an immediate biological family member alive in their home country.

For adopted children who had no knowledge or memory of their past, I found that the more information adoptive parents could glean about their children's history, the better; it proved beneficial in helping the children grasp their identity. Often this information is not readily available at the time of adoption, and some families find that they need to use other methods to learn more about their children's history, sometimes at a later date.

I once talked to an adoptive parent who told me that knowing the details of their children's history was unimportant, as their kids seemed to want to forget the past. Though I can sympathize with wanting to help children from a difficult past make a fresh start, I've observed that simply ignoring the past is rarely helpful, and sooner or later, it will have to be dealt with. Understanding their history allows those who are adopted to work through their stories so that they can experience healing and wholeness.

Megan, one of the adoptive mothers I interviewed, shared how her family hired a private investigator in Ukraine who helped them search for their three daughters' biological families in order to gain details of the children's histories. Their search uncovered a biological brother of one of the adopted daughters. The brother had been adopted to the US years before. The connection provided significant information and family background for their daughter. "I'm glad we did the family searches, especially as the girls got older," Megan said. "I think it's wrong for kids to forget their identity and where they came from." She also said the information they gathered has answered questions for their children, and as a result, the past is no longer a veiled mystery. She believes this element has been crucial in their healing journeys.

Some families opted to return to Ukraine several years after the adoption in order to search for relatives and old friends. Sometimes the return to Ukraine coincided with the adoption of additional children. I've often been asked when it's appropriate for an adopted child to visit a home country as a part of a journey to understanding the past. Though there's no magical age or time frame, I have observed that some kids return too soon. I think such a visit should be done only after several years and after more secure attachments have formed between adoptive parents and children. The return to their home country can be a healing process for some children—if it's done at the right age and if they're feeling secure in their new home. For kids who are still struggling to attach and find their identity in a new culture, a return too soon can actually cause more trauma and confusion and can trigger old behaviors.

Help Kids Understand Brain Development

Stephanie and Ryan adopted two sisters, ages six and eight when they brought them home. One thing they found to be helpful on the healing journey was providing education for their daughters about how childhood events can impact brain development.

> When we learned about early childhood brain development, it was revolutionary to us, so we introduced the idea of the neurological aspect of their development to our girls, to help them better understand their brains and why they do what they

do. They're very inquisitive about stuff like that. The more info they have from us, the better. Once we understood that trust is formed in the early years of maternal nurture, we explained to them that their brother, our biological child, never had to learn to trust like they have. Our daughter Alana, who is most interested in learning, has even been able to take ownership in understanding her own condition. Now she wants to study it on her own in order to understand herself better. She's actually asked for books for Christmas to better understand her brain. Who asks for books about your traumatized brain for Christmas? That's our daughter. She's a processor.

I recognize this isn't the case for all adoptees, and perhaps some children or teens lack the cognitive ability to compute all the implications surrounding brain development, but I found what this couple shared to be very enlightening. Our conversation reminded me of another conversation I had with a young adult adoptee I've known for many years. Mary was adopted around the age of eight and, for the most part, transitioned well into family life. Her family had three other children, and Mary became the youngest. From what her parents shared with me, Mary had some issues around attachment and bonding, and in her preteen years she had a limited capacity to develop meaningful or lasting friendships.

When I met with Mary a couple of months ago, she was twenty-one and had just completed her second year of college. She shared with me about a psychology class she was taking where she was learning about adult attachment styles. As a result of her studies, she was beginning to really understand herself for the first time. She said it was as if she had been given a lens through which to see the ways her early childhood experiences were playing into her relationship problems as an adult.

I remember when Mary was in elementary school, so to be having this conversation with her and seeing her making mature assessments of her life was a joy and privilege. I could see the light bulbs coming on for her as she connected concrete knowledge about her attachment style to areas where she had struggled. As she was processing the information, she was recognizing the need to learn skills to overcome her areas of weakness so that she could maintain healthy relationships in the future. All adoptive parents desire for their children to have similar revelations so they can see themselves through new eyes and take their own steps toward healing.

Consider Trust-Based Relational Intervention (TBRI)

One of the most popular and widely read books on the topic of adoptive parenting is *The Connected Child* by Karyn Purvis, David Cross, and Wendy Lyons Sunshine. The book and its methodology were referenced by fifteen of the families I interviewed, some saying the material was the lifeline they needed in a desperate time and others finding it less helpful, or not helpful at all. Drs. Purvis and Cross developed TBRI (Trust-Based Relational Intervention) at

Texas Christian University. According to the Karyn Purvis Institute of Child Development website, "TBRI is an attachment-based, trauma-informed intervention designed to meet the complex needs of vulnerable children. TBRI uses Empowering Principles to address physical needs, Connecting Principles for attachment needs, and Correcting Principles to disarm fear-based behaviors. While the intervention is based on years of attachment, sensory processing, and neuroscience research, the central aim of TBRI is connection."[2]

Recently I was able to be a part of the team that translated and published *The Connected Child* into the Russian language in Ukraine. It is material I have long been familiar with and have recommended to many adoptive families, so I was curious to see how families actually utilized the principles and where they saw the strategies effective.

Brandon and Marcy Jones shared that using the TBRI principles helped them reach and better understand their daughters. "We got all of Karyn Purvis's DVDs and books before we adopted, and when we had our girls it suddenly became, 'Which video do we need to watch tonight?' " Brandon said. "The teaching of Karyn Purvis was a lifeline and changed how I dealt with our girls. It helped us get them to succeed when a crisis happens, which has been huge. Her work helped me to prepare to interact with them, otherwise I would have fallen back on how my dad parented, which was yelling and screaming. I can see when I escalate and now understand there is no purpose in that."

His wife, Marcy, added, "The material also gave me a better understanding of kids who have been through trauma and how you can't parent them the way you'd parent other children. It helped me understand how their brains were affected, and if they learn to trust and have a safe environment the chemistry in their brains can change. I see how they were operating in the orphanage and how they were living in a stress zone, and it takes time for their bodies and brains to relearn."

Reading *The Connected Child* helped Lynn and her husband, Ben, who are parenting six older adopted kids from Ukraine. Lynn shared that learning the TBRI principles was the only thing that worked with one of their adopted sons. "We saw a lot of growth in our kids when we started using concepts found in the book. We've taught all our kids about trauma. We've tried to help them understand why they act the way they do—what is going on in their brains. Helping our oldest understand why he self-soothes was helpful. But it was really hard to retrain ourselves and stop the way we'd been parenting before."

Another family, the Ericksons, had middle-school-aged children at home when they adopted their first daughter, and over the course of several years they added three more children from Ukraine to their family. Each of their children presented unique challenges, so the Ericksons, too, looked to the wisdom of Karyn Purvis's teaching when seeking to help their children. "We tried our best to apply Karyn Purvis's principles and lower our expectations. We learned quickly it's totally different parenting children who come from brokenness. With our son, we tried everything, and nothing helped. With our daughter, therapy techniques we learned from Karyn Purvis helped, like learning different calming techniques like bouncing on a trampoline. Our journey was about learning and understanding that different methods worked with different children. We are always open to trying new things to get our kids the help they need."

Help Kids Conquer Shame

Kerri, an adoptive mother of two preteens, had another encouraging story to share about how her daughter, Laura, had some breakthroughs when she was finally able to understand and express the concept of shame.

> Laura would often say things like, "You don't know what I am, you don't know what I've done. When I look in the mirror, I see a monster." There was so much shame in her and around her, you could feel it, it was palpable. And then one night we were watching *Kung Fu Panda*, and there's this part in the movie where the word shame comes up. And Laura said, "Aha—that's the word I want." It struck me as odd that she resonated with that word. But then she would use it—to shame herself, her sister, or to even shame us for different things.
>
> I realized I needed to go to the Lord about this. So one night I prayed with the girls and said, "Lord,

thank You that on the cross You took away all our shame, and we don't have any shame anymore because You took it all on a shameful cross, and we have Your life in us now, and we are no longer under any shame." And you know, I didn't hear any more about shame or the word even used in a sentence after I prayed that prayer. It was literally like a light bulb went on for her and she heard what I was saying—what God was saying. I think it was a huge healing moment.

Help Kids Build Trust

Shannon, adoptive mother of Ana, a preteen, shared about a healing moment she had with her daughter as she gave Ana permission to be honest about her negative feelings.

There was a time over a year ago when she was really angry at me and she said, "Sometimes I just want to leave and go live with someone else." I tried to feel her out to see what she meant. The conversation ended and I gave her a little bit of time to be by herself. Then I went upstairs to her room and said, "It's okay that you hate me right now." When I said that, she looked at me like I was crazy. I went on to tell her there was a time when I hated my parents, too, and even told them that. I told her that her current feelings would likely change if she gave it time, and that I wasn't going anywhere.

After that conversation she seemed freer, and it seemed she no longer felt as though she had to keep it all together all the time and keep her feelings inside. A wall came down. Since then she's been a real kid. It was a pivotal moment in our relationship. She doesn't hide stuff anymore because she knows she doesn't need to. She finally understands and trusts that we aren't going any-where.

Like Shannon experienced with Ana, Landon and Nora have endured a long journey to see their adopted teenage son find healing and learn to trust that they will always be there for him. Landon shared:

He had the attitude of, "There's no way you're going to love me forever, so I'm going to check out now before you check out on me." We never gave up on him, and I think he finally has started to see we aren't going anywhere. He'd been disappointed so many times, so he expected to be disappointed by us. There was a time when he'd run away from our home and later came to the door and expressed an interest in coming back. I told him if he was going to return, he was going to have to live by our rules. He wasn't sure if he was ready for that. So, he left again. Then, a while later, he came back and once again asked to come home. I kept telling him the same thing, "*We* never left you. *You* walked out the door." I made sure I kept telling him that, that he understood who left. I must have told him that about ten times.

Finally, when he came back in a broken state and was ready to stay, he said, "I'm sorry for leaving you." I think he finally realized that although no one had been permanent in his life, we were here to stay, and he could come to us. He is now finally at a point in his life where he is willing to receive help.

Consider Supporting Kids with Therapy

Of the adoptive families I surveyed, 55 percent said they'd sought out counseling or psychotherapy for themselves as individuals or as a couple. Seventy-four percent said that their child(ren) had received counseling or therapy after being adopted. In some cases, this benefitted both parents and children. However, of the 74 percent, only 5.8 percent said they had seen significant benefits of therapy for their child. Forty-nine percent said they had seen some benefits, and 17 percent said they saw little to no benefits. Many said the biggest challenge was keeping their children going to counseling, as kids and teens would refuse to return after several sessions. These parents felt the sessions were not worth the cost if the children weren't willing to talk and work through things. The hope remained that when the kids were ready to talk about their feelings, counseling could be a viable method of healing.

One family I interviewed near the end of my journey shared about a therapy their children underwent that proved radically helpful in the healing process. The Jacksons adopted their children, siblings Anton and Lily, at the ages of ten and seven respectively. They knew their son Anton had witnessed some horrific events at a young age, and as he transitioned into their home, it was clear he had significant issues with anger and rage.

After a couple of years in his new home, Anton was diagnosed with post-traumatic stress disorder (PTSD). His mom, Maggie, shared, "He literally couldn't process life the same way you or I process things. It was like he was only seeing through a pinhole. The doctor explained it would be like driving while looking through two small tubes, unable to process all that was passing by and instead reacting only to what you see directly in front of you. The doctor explained that Anton was always in fight-or-flight mode, so when certain things would happen, his anger would get triggered, and he would rage because adrenaline was coursing through his body."

After consulting with other adoptive families and considering numerous options, the Jacksons learned of a form of light therapy called "Fight or Flight,"[3] which involves looking at a bright light for twenty minutes twice a day. Curtis, Anton's dad, said they were very skeptical about the treatment when they first began to look into it, but after listening to several families who testified to its success, they decided it was worth a try.

Within a month, they had a radically different child in their home. "The light therapy gave him the tools he needed to be able to process things normally," Maggie said. "Before, he would just snap when we would point out a behavior. But once his perception changed, you could actually see him make a choice, like to stay calm, whereas before it was clear he wasn't capable of making that choice. He had to sit and stare into the light for twenty minutes at a time, but at least he was willing to do it."

Now the Jacksons feel they can communicate with Anton at a different level and that he is able to receive correction from them, which he was unable to do before the light therapy. Their daughter Lily also did sessions of light therapy. The Jacksons explained that Lily was very introverted and couldn't express herself, but through the therapy she gained the ability to verbalize her thoughts and emotions.

The Jacksons are the only family I'm aware of among those I interviewed who tried this particular form of therapy. Because they noticed such drastic behavioral changes in their son, and their daughter also benefited, I decided it was worth noting in this text. I hope parents who have children with similar challenges might potentially be helped by this information.

I recognize that therapies and counselors are an additional financial burden for many, but continuing to explore various avenues of professional assistance can be very important. Sometimes it takes time to find the right fit for a specific child or situation, and some families said they looked into therapy for a child who they ultimately decided wasn't ready to process or receive help. However, other parents advised that families ought to budget counseling into their adoption expenses so they can get extra help for their children when the time is right.

Seek Healing through Christ

As discussed in the chapter about spiritual warfare, many families felt prayer and the Word of God brought the most healing to their children. Nothing is more powerful in the transformation process than the work of Jesus Himself in the hearts of adopted children.

I observed a big difference in homes where the adopted kids had sincerely accepted Jesus as Lord of their lives and were allowing Him into their broken places. I saw much healing taking place in the lives of kids who were pursuing God at a deep level.

In some of the homes I visited, corporate Bible reading and prayer were central to daily family life. In other homes there were fewer collective family activities centered on their faith, but there was more focus on each individual pursuing God. The majority of the families I interviewed self-identified as evangelical Christians and were active in a local church. These parents hoped and prayed their children would come to a faith in Christ on their own, and some required their teens to attend church or youth group. In other homes, parents left the decision about church attendance up to their teen adoptees, not wanting to force anything or to make church a point of contention.

Roger Clark, a pastor with adopted teens, said that although he prayed constantly for his kids, he was careful not to push his family's faith on his adopted children because of his role as a pastor.

> We haven't pushed any of our kids to accept our faith, but we have watched each of them desire to learn more. I told my son, "You really need to listen on Sundays so you can get some of your questions answered." I was fearful that if I started asking him if he was ready to receive Christ, he would do it just to make me happy. . . . I really wanted him to come to the Lord on his own.
>
> One day recently he said, "Dad, I want to know more about God."
>
> I said, "What do you mean by that?"
>
> He answered, "I want to be His son."
>
> And I was like, "Wow, that's pretty big!"
>
> We talked more and I didn't push him. A few days later, he came back and said, "So how do I get saved? I want to be saved." I reminded him of the story of Nicodemus and what it means to inherit the kingdom of God. We prayed together, and he started on his journey with Jesus that day.

On the other hand, one of our daughters still wrestles with Christianity. She says, "I spent fifteen years in an orphanage. Why did God allow that? Why did He take so long to get me out?" We tell her we don't know all the answers. We just keep praying she'll see how God can use it all, if she lets Him.

One Size Does Not Fit All

I am reminded how God deals with us holistically and ministers to us individually. We have to remember that a child's journey to healing will be unique and likely multi-faceted. God can administer healing in so many different ways and on a timeline very different than ours. Sometimes we are tempted to approach healing as though it's purely spiritual or purely emotional or purely neurological when, in reality, we must keep in mind how God created us and the multidimensional way we all can, and do, experience healing.

Recently I was listening to a sermon by Pastor Tim Keller that illustrated this point of how we tend to focus on only one part of a person instead of realizing each person has many facets. Keller used the story of Elijah, found in chapter nineteen of 1 Kings, to make this connection. This is the famous chapter in which the prophet Elijah has just victoriously slain the prophets of Baal but is now running in fear from Jezebel, who is out to kill him.

Elijah is broken and worn down, and he finds refuge under a broom tree, where he's ready to curl up and die.

It's there that the Lord sends an angel to minister to Elijah, and the first thing the angel does is provide food (vv. 5–6). As Keller explained in his sermon, "God treats this depressed man with a multidisciplinary approach. He treats him understanding all the dimensions in which he lives. He's a physical being, he's a relational being, he's a spiritual being. . . . The first thing He does is He cooks, the second thing He does with Elijah, if you look carefully, is He listens. . . . The third thing God does is He says, 'You need to spend time with My Word; you need to listen to My voice, you need to listen to My Word, you need to come into My presence,' because we do have a spiritual nature."[4]

In today's world, we are tempted to reduce our struggles to just one aspect of our nature. Keller shared how some people focus only on the physical, so when they come upon a depressed or hurting person, they want to find a chemical answer. Their response to the person struggling emotionally is, "Take a pill, and all will be well."

Another group of people, Keller's so-called "moralists," reduces everything to a spiritual level. These are the people who conclude that if there's something not right, then there's something wrong in someone's spiritual life—a hidden sin or not enough prayer. It's difficult to get the moralist to take a pill for anything.

The third group reduces everything to the psychological, that people just need counseling and to talk things out in order to get better. They say people shouldn't be judged or evaluated but simply allowed to discover who they are.

Keller summarized these three views by saying, "When a worldview reduces everything to the physical, reduces everything to the spiritual, reduces everything to the psychological, it's not going to deal with real problems. If you try to reduce everything, you're not going to really deal with the complexity of reality, you're not really going to help people. But the God of the Bible never does such a thing. Because the God of the Bible has . . . not only invented body, soul, and spirit but He's *redeeming* them all."[5]

I see how we can be tempted to compartmentalize healing the way Keller described. We may think that only the right therapy or the right medication or the right prayer offered by the right healing minister will set a child free. I believe these various attempts simply point to the fact that parents long for their children to find healing.

A couple of years ago in Ukraine, we held our biannual Strengthening Families Conference for Ukrainian adoptive families, and we used the concept of *kintsugi* as the theme for our conference. Kintsugi is an ancient form of Japanese artwork by which a broken piece of pottery is repaired using a lacquer mixed with powdered gold, silver, or platinum. The end result is a work of art that is worth far more than the original pottery.

Throughout our weekend, we unpacked what it means to be mended with gold as we allow God into our broken places. One beautiful aspect of kintsugi is that no two pieces are alike. Even if you had two identical pieces of pottery when they were whole, once they're broken, they'll be broken in different places, thus mended in unique ways.

From the time I first became aware of kintsugi, I was struck by the parallels to how adopted children find healing. Just like a piece of broken pottery, every child will be mended and healed in a different way.

For some families, they have noted healing when their child confesses something without being asked. For others, it's a moment when a child who would've previously melted down or exploded in anger instead makes a choice to defuse the situation. For some children, healing means being able to receive affection or willing to accept help. Sometimes healing is one step forward, followed by three steps back. There is no magical timeline for the healing process. The "little" breakthroughs are often bigger than a family realizes at the time.

"When my daughter cries in front of me, that's the high-light of my day because when she came to us, she didn't have access to her emotions, let alone her tears," shared one adoptive mother. "When she lets us in and receives our help, I begin to see a glimpse of the healing to come, and that's the hope I hold on to."

For Reflection or Group Discussion

1. Are there any little ways you have seen growth or healing in your adopted child, if you have adopted?

2. Which story in this chapter was the most encouraging to you personally? Why?

3. If you have adopted, which aspect of your child's healing do you feel you have placed the most emphasis on: physical, psychological, emotional, social, or spiritual? Which area do you think has been most neglected?

4. Are there any changes you want to make in your own life after reading this chapter? Please explain.

10

Rest Stops and Treasure Shops

Faith Lessons in Adoption

More than anything, I now step back and see God's finger-prints on this process. This was never supposed to be easy and yet I've learned God loves us in the middle of our glorious mess. All of us.

—ADOPTIVE MOTHER

"If you want to know how much of a sinner you are, go and adopt children." I heard this sentiment repeatedly throughout my interviews. Although it might have been said rather tongue in cheek, more than one parent intimated, "Adopting a child is sanctification on steroids!"

Based on what parents shared, I could draw an imaginary pyramid of sanctification "steps" leading upward in these couples' lives. Marriage would be the first step of sanctification, parenting the second step, parenting toddlers and teens the third, and adopting children yet another step closer to understanding their need for a Savior.

As noted in earlier chapters, the majority of the families I spoke with adopted in faith and obedience to what they'd deemed a calling or leading from God. Many of these families shared the ways they have grown in their faith as a result of adopting. But adopting children also revealed to these parents that they still had a lot to learn about their own character and, even more important, about the character and love of God.

Blessing Redefined

Michael, an adoptive parent of two teenage siblings, said, "We think of blessings as gifts, right? We talk about adoption as a blessing. But many would ask, 'How are two traumatized kids a gift?' We took a big risk in bringing these kids home. When you face adversity, it challenges you and changes you. . . . The experience of adoption will either break you or make you stronger. Before we did this, I honestly didn't understand the level of brokenness that kids could have. Through my kids, God has opened my eyes to the pain in many children that I otherwise wouldn't have noticed. I see this now as a blessing of knowledge."

Bethany, who adopted her son Vanya when he was fourteen, shared about how God has used him to teach her more about herself and God, particularly in regard to the difference between conditional and unconditional love. "I have struggled with loving people unconditionally," she said. "There have been times when Vanya has been very hard to love, but God asks me to love him as he is. Something happens and we fight, and maybe I want to hate him, but I have to wake up the next morning and make his breakfast. I've seen Vanya grow in loving me too. We had a conflict about something recently, and on his own he apologized to me and later brought me flowers. I've seen him grow in his ability to forgive as well."

The Kaiser family was fascinating for me to observe in action. The parents, Tara and Ron, have eight children, four with varying degrees of special needs. Their family life is an interesting combination of highly structured and laid back. In their home, I saw both an established rhythm and a peaceful simplicity. Though Tara and Ron are honest about the struggles they've faced with their children, they choose to focus on the blessings more than the burdens that adoption has added to their lives.

When I asked what they've learned most about God throughout their journey of adoption, they spoke of the Lord's faithfulness and provision. Tara said,

> We've seen how God has shown up time and time again. Part of what I love about the adoption life that God has given us is what it has taught our biological children about the Lord and His faithfulness and provision. We adopted four kids in a short period of time, and God provided every penny we needed. We're not typically budgeters, but when we'd occasionally review our finances, we would see that we were spending more than we were making. Yet, we never ran out of money. I don't

understand how the math worked, but there was always enough in the account, so we stopped trying to figure it out. We knew somehow the Lord was providing.

We've also had a supportive network of fellow adoptive families. There are a lot of adopted children in our kids' school. My kids have no idea that it's not typical to have adopted children in a family. They have friends who've also had challenging siblings in their homes, so they understand one another. We're now equipped to support other parents in our community and have seen our testimony lead others to adopt. I've seen the sacrifices my children have made and the love they're able to give to their siblings. People with a different perspective think we're cheating our kids because we have less financially, but we see how we're blessing our kids. When we first told our own parents we were adopting, they thought it was so unwise. They were completely unsupportive. But now that time has passed, my mom would give her right arm for our children. Seeing that transformation has been amazing. We've seen God everywhere in this process.

Marcus, a father who admittedly struggled in feeling emotionally connected to his adopted son, shared about the unexpected blessings adoption has brought him, particularly in regard to what it revealed in his own heart.

"I've gained a new understanding of how ugly I can be toward God and so full of sin, yet He still loves me. We do things that displease Him, yet when we turn to Him, He forgives us. I've learned there's a misconception in our culture that obedience equals a particular kind of blessing. Perhaps obedience does equal blessing, but not always blessing in a way we want or perceive. Being obedient and faithful in this adoption, even in the hard times, has been my offering of worship to God."

Amazing Grace

Cara has learned important lessons from her adopted son as well. "Having Sam has shown me how much I need God because I'm not as good as I thought I was. If a little kid with an accent can push my buttons, then I'm not as 'chill' as I once thought. This has shown me how much I need the Father; how much I need His grace."

Jessica, another adoptive mom, spoke about the ways she's had to take ownership of her own sinfulness rather than blaming her challenges on her child's issues or behaviors. The adoption of her son has had her reflect on her own flaws as if looking in a mirror, and in these moments, she has been reminded to go to the Lord with her emotions. "There was this one time when I was at church and I was about to take communion. I started to ask for forgiveness about my anger that had been building toward my son," she recalled. "So many times I would think, 'My son makes me *so* angry.' But the Holy Spirit spoke clearly to my heart and I felt so convicted about my attitude. 'Yes, your son does bad things,' I felt the Lord whisper, 'but it's *your* anger.' Suddenly, I got it. I can't control *his* behavior, but I can control *my* reactions. For three years I was an angry mom, but in that moment, I realized that I need to be a better steward of my emotions and not give in so easily to anger and blame." In doing so, Jessica has come to appreciate God's grace at a whole new level.

Nancy and Matthew had already raised four children when they adopted a teenage boy, and then several years later, they were able to adopt his younger sister as well. Matthew shared, "I had to learn I couldn't take their behavior personally—it wasn't about me." His wife, Nancy, added, "The biggest thing God has shown me is I have to guard my heart from idolizing my kids and keep God on the throne. I've had to recognize, motherhood *can't* be the ultimate source of my joy. I also had to let go of my pride and relinquish my idea of being the 'perfect' family. God has shown me I'm more useful to Him with my cracks and brokenness, and His grace covers it all."

Ethan and Brenda, whose adopted teenage son left their home for a season and had recently returned at the time of the interview, explained the ways their relationship with him has helped them understand God's view of His children. Brenda said,

> I had this tendency to think, "When I rebel, God must be so tired of me." But even with what we've been through with our son, we still want him back. We don't write him off, and we keep the door open

for him. It's easy to get in a pattern of thinking that says, "God could write us off if we turn our back on Him." That's how my earthly father was, so I've been inclined to attribute that characteristic to God. But God isn't at all like that, and this adoption has helped me to tangibly experience a tiny piece of God's heart in a new way. I see now how God is patient. He's always ready to take me back.

Ethan added, "I've learned how tenacious God's love and grace are. There are moments I want to strangle my son and other times I'd take a bullet for him. I understand God's love more because I see how He gives us everything, and yet sometimes we spit in His face. I see how our rebellion must hurt Him, and yet at the same time how patient He is with us."

Carol, whose adopted daughter Katya had been home for four years at the time of the interview, shared, "Because of my daughter, I have a better understanding of the sacrifice Jesus made for us. I have an understanding of the lost sheep, and that the Shepherd left the ninety-nine for the one. It's a parable, yes, but it's a beautiful picture of what Jesus did for us. The one lamb was precious to Him. God's heart is always tender toward his children."

Compassion for Others

Janet, an adoptive mom who has parented a child with significant behavior issues, shared how she now sees other parents who are struggling with new eyes. "My compassion for moms who have children with behavior problems has grown. Before I adopted, I used to think, 'Do you not discipline your child?' Now I see a mom in a bad situation with her child throwing a tantrum and I just say, 'What do you need? I have one, too, so I understand.'"

"It's very convicting to adopt," said Tammy, an adoptive mother of one. "You like to think of yourself as 'nonjudgmental' as a Christian, but oh boy, the things you can think on the inside, like, 'Oh I would *never* do things the way that person does.' But we never *really* know what another family is experiencing or how dark it can be. Through adopting you learn to have compassion and grace for people you were judging before. It's been interesting to switch places and realize, *we* are now the family who's probably being judged."

Aaron, who early on struggled in forming an attachment to his adopted son, shared, "I've become more sensitive to people who are hurting. I understand people's struggles better now, and I'm no longer dismissive of other people's feelings, nor do I try to fix how they feel. I also understand the effects of long-term sadness and crisis." His wife, Dana, added, "I've seen my own shortcomings in such a big way. I used to be so judgmental of people and think they should be able to just snap out of certain emotions. But I see how sin and negative feelings can really get a hold on you and how alone you can feel. Today I have much more compassion for people and understand how healing takes time."

Redemptive Suffering

I've spoken about how people like happy endings and struggle with stories that haven't yet resolved in what we would consider a positive light. Many families I interviewed, however, have learned to bear suffering with great courage, even when it doesn't seem to make sense.

Gina and her husband, Tim, adopted their son when he was eight. Kostya had gone through significant trauma in his early life with his birth parents as well as in the orphanage where he was placed. From the very beginning, this couple knew they would be walking a challenging road in helping Kostya integrate into their family.

Gina shared a powerful illustration about what God has taught her through the adoption:

> We always try to find a reason for our suffering, but sometimes it doesn't seem to have a constructive purpose except for being with Christ in *His* suffering. If I can offer my suffering to Christ, as in, "I'm going to suffer this without complaint because You suffered for me," I can give my suffering meaning, which can help me deal with it. Protestants are really bad about this. We want to glibly quote Romans 8:28: "Everything will work together for good." We want to rush to find out, "What's the good that's going to come out of this?" But sometimes the good isn't a tangible thing. Sometimes the good is simply that you've humbled yourself. I can offer my discomforts up to God,

and that can redeem and give purpose to my suffering.

I think of Mary, who held things in her heart yet they cut like a sword. I identify with Mary so much. I'm certainly not the only mother who has suffered and struggled, asking "What does this mean? Why is this happening? Why is this *so* hard?" If I can offer my anger and my suffering and my heartbreak to God, then He can redeem it. That makes the sacrifices less difficult to bear.

When they were in their twenties, Aubrey and Joe felt called by God to adopt a baby boy with Down syndrome. When I first met this young couple in Ukraine, I was amazed at their faith and conviction in what God had called them to do so early on in their lives and marriage. Seeing them six years later, I was impressed at the perspective they'd gained through the unique challenges they'd taken on.

"God has taught me so much about sacrifice," Aubrey said, "to truly love without strings attached and without receiving anything in return."

Joe agreed. "This whole process has been the perfect display of Christ on the cross," he said. "When we were contemplating adopting a child with Down syndrome, we made a list of all the pros and cons and what it could mean for our lives. Everything on the pro side was only spiritual enhancement, and everything on the con list was all around fleshly or selfish desires. Looking at that list was like examining our hearts. But then I looked at the sacrifice that Jesus made for us. He made the choice to give up everything, including his royalty, for *us*. He took our shame. Of course, the picture of the sacrifice became a lot more real after the years passed in caring for our son. . . . But we made the choice to make him ours."

Aubrey added, "This was always God's plan for us. I wouldn't have made this choice for myself to adopt a son with Down syndrome, and that's how I know it was the Holy Spirit leading and not just us. Above all, I've learned to keep pressing into what's hard and not run from it. [Jesus] can redeem it all, even when we don't see how."

Perseverance

At a conference I helped organize for adoptive families last year, Cindy, who adopted her daughter over twenty years ago, shared her story of perseverance over two decades of parenting. Hers is a message of hope for adoptive families who find themselves in the middle of a battle and tempted to give up.

From the limited information Cindy and her husband, Craig, had about their adopted daughter, Anastasia, they knew she'd experienced significant trauma in her young life. Anastasia was four years old and had been in the orphanage for a little over a year when they brought her home to their family. "That first night," Cindy said, "I wanted her close, so I tucked her in a little bed next to me for the night. I was later awakened by sad, quiet, moaning sounds that seemed to be coming from deep inside her. I suddenly envisioned her in horrible pain and suffering, like a terrified little animal caught in a hunter's trap. This frightened me. 'God,' I said silently, 'How will I ever help a little girl who has this much pain?' "

Years passed, and in addition to Anastasia and their two biological children, Cindy and Craig had one more biological daughter. Cindy admitted she and Craig knew very little, if anything, about the effects of trauma or attachment disorder in the early years of parenting their children. They were on the earlier side of the international adoption boom and found themselves with few resources, and they lacked a community of other adoptive families. They parented Anastasia the best way they knew and kept praying God would heal the broken places in her heart that were becoming more apparent as she grew.

Cindy was often frustrated by the challenging behaviors that were surfacing in her daughter, but then she would bring to mind the image of the frightened animal being caught in the trap. This helped her remember what she was struggling against.

> When Anastasia became a teenager, her deepest emotions rose to the surface, and I didn't know how to respond to the anger, rebellion, and self-harm she displayed. We felt we'd completely failed her as parents. My heart felt crushed and rejected. I believed that God was at work, and I understood this was His plan for us to go through—but for how long?

While we were walking through a particularly painful season with our daughter, God gave me a profound dream. In my dream, my youngest daughter, who'd always been a gentle, peaceful presence in our home, was once again a young child and out on a bicycle ride. In the dream, a gang of men caught her, beat her, and raped her. I found her limp body, physically alive but emotionally dead. Picking her up in my arms, I felt so much love and knew in my innermost being that I'd give her love for the rest of my life and care for her however she needed. When I awoke from that awful dream, I understood God wanted me to know that the emotions I was feeling for my biological daughter were the emotions He felt toward my adopted daughter, *His* daughter, Anastasia. It was a sobering awakening.

I continued trying to build a relationship with Anastasia, but by the time she left home as a young adult, there was no bond of affection, and she stayed connected only by her need for money in desperate times. My husband kept reaching out to her, but I felt like I had nothing left to give.

When she was twenty-three, we were presented with an opportunity to attend a camp that focused on reconciling hurting family relationships. The time at the camp was very hard. It was clear Anastasia had no intention of connecting with me.

At the end of the first day, I collapsed in tears and decided I couldn't stay. I had to get out of there and was set to go home the next day.

But that night, as I lay awake, I felt the Lord speak to my heart: "Do you remember the hunter's trap?"

I answered, "Yes, for the thousandth time, *I remember.*"

Then again, I felt Him saying, "And do you remember how you felt toward your youngest daughter when she had been hurt in your dream?"

I said again, "Yes, Lord. But *I hurt too much.* I just can't take more."

I heard in my spirit, "What if that had been your *youngest* daughter caught in the hunter's trap? What if she was lashing out at you and anyone trying to free her? What would you do for *her?*"

Tears streamed down my face as I pictured the situation and immediately knew what I would do. "I'd let her kill me before I ever stopped trying to free her from the trap."

Then, oh so softly, so tenderly, so meekly, the Lord asked me one more question. "Will you do this for Anastasia? Will you do it for Me? Will you keep fighting?"

I awoke that next morning knowing I wouldn't leave the camp. I'd stay, keep trying, and listen to what Anastasia had to say. The rest of the week was far from easy, but I remained. On the last day, we were told to stand face to face with our child and give her a compliment. Looking into my daughter's angry and glaring eyes, I chose to look beyond her anger, and in faith I said to her, "Under all this anger, I know you love your family, and I know someday we will be best friends."

In an unexpectedly vulnerable moment, she looked at me and said, "You are the strongest woman I know. You've given everything for your family. You're also the most forgiving person I know."

I felt like she said this with sincerity, and her words were a glimmer of hope that something was getting through. More lessons were yet to be learned, but I will say that today, four years after that experience, we have come a long way in our relationship. The adoption journey can be a long one, and we need to be wise in the boundaries we set with our children to keep us protected and emotionally well. But we have to keep going and continue fighting for them. The battle is the Lord's, and His victory comes in His timing.

Diamonds in the Rough

When I began gathering these various treasures—spiritual and life lessons learned in adoption— I kept in mind the idiom "diamonds in the rough" because I thought it had a nice ring to it.

I reasoned that adoption is often challenging, and yet in the rockiness of the process, we can discover gems.

As I thought more about this idiom and its meaning, I decided to do my own bit of digging on diamonds—figuratively, that is—and read about the process of how a rock is turned into a girl's best friend. It's a complicated process with multiple steps involved. To extract the diamond from the rock and transform it into the gem on display in the jewelry store takes time. I read in one source, "The goal of gem-cutting is to form a beautiful, polished stone. In the case of transparent gemstones, you want to maximize two qualities: fire and brilliance. Fire is the ability of a stone to fracture light into rainbows, much as a prism does. Brilliance is the amount of white light reflected back out of the stone. A poor cut can lead to poor fire and brilliance."[1]

Those last two words struck me. Every diamond contains a different amount of fire and brilliance, all depending on how the diamond is uniquely cut. Reading that, I couldn't help but think of the families represented in the pages of this book and the faith lessons illustrated in this chapter. These parents allowed God into their adoption story and, in the process, offered themselves up to be cut and shaped. Like diamonds, each one discovered varying degrees of fire and brilliance in themselves when placed into the chiseling hand of the Father.

On a recent trip to Atlanta, I stayed with Susan, a colleague of mine, whose family adopted eight children from Russia in the '90s. The kids were between the ages of eight and fourteen at the different times they were adopted, and today they are adults in their mid-twenties and mid-thirties. The family has experienced their fair share of ups and downs, but as the kids have walked into adulthood, Susan and her husband, Brian, have seen immense break-throughs. Their family's journey of over two decades helped put so many of the stories I had heard into perspective.

Susan shared that the hardest years of struggle and war-fare for their children's destinies came when they were between the ages of eighteen to twenty-five. But even in the darkest moments, when the kids were far from home (literally and figuratively) and far from God, Susan and her husband continued to demonstrate to their kids that they were available and would not stop loving them. Sometimes that love was from a distance, and sometimes that love meant taking a daughter and her prostitute friends out for a warm meal.

As Susan told her story, she shared some of the revela-tions God laid on her heart to help her love and serve her children while they were continuing to live with orphan spirits. Susan likes to call this her "middle-of-the-night, six-point sermon." These points correlate with what God spoke to His people through the prophet Ezekiel.

1. *Speak truth,* even if they don't listen. (Ezekiel 2:7)

2. *Seek God,* taking time away to be in His presence. (Ezekiel 1:1, 28)

3. *Surgery is needed* on your heart and on theirs, as *both* have become hardened. (Ezekiel 11:19)

4. *Salvation comes* when your response is based on who God is, not how you feel. (Ezekiel 20:4, 9)

5. *Shepherding,* not badgering, is what your children need. (Ezekiel 34:1)

6. *Spiritual life* supernaturally transforms. (Ezekiel 37:4)

When everything felt too hard, Susan went back to these faith lessons that the Lord had whispered to her heart through His Word, and she rested in those instructions on how to keep loving and staying present in the lives of her children. As Susan likes to say to encourage other battle-weary parents, "Remember, what you're seeing right now is *just* a video clip. This is *not* the entire movie."

For Reflection or Group Discussion

1. As you read the various faith lessons shared in this chapter, which lessons did you most relate to? Why?

2. What is the most brilliant truth you have learned about God on your adoption journey or in your life, if you have not adopted?

3. What is an insight or gem you have realized about your own personality through your adoption experience or the experience of someone you know?

11

Limited Visibility

The Journey Continues

Difficult roads often lead to beautiful destinations.

—*ZIG ZIGLAR*

W hen I started out on this journey of capturing post-adoption experiences, I wasn't sure how it would all come together. It sounded like great fun and an adventure of epic proportions when the book and road trip were only abstract concepts in my mind, but as the time drew closer to start the journey, the reality of what I was taking on began to sink in, and it was more than a little scary.

Days before hitting the road, I recall lying in bed and anxiously wondering how could I possibly do this. Several months later, as I drove up Interstate 5 and crossed the Washington border, where I had begun, I thought to myself, "Wow! It actually happened. It's finished!" Then the next paralyzing thought hit me: "How are you ever going to summarize all these interviews and write a book?" The talking part was fun, but processing it all and making sense of what I heard seemed like an insurmountable task. How could I take the stories of sixty-three families and give an accurate representation of what they experienced?

People tend to ask me the same question about what I discovered through listening to so many post-adoption stories. "So, were the adoptions you witnessed successful?" People want a simple answer. Yes or no? Good or bad? Proceed or halt?

I've tried not to let the question offend me, as I understand it's asked with sincere curiosity and maybe a bit of naivety—or perhaps the asker just wants hard data to know which way the pendulum swings most often. But the question always unsettles me nonetheless, maybe because I, too, have been tempted to categorize adoption stories. I've wanted easy answers and quick conclusions. I've wanted to put labels on people's stories so they'd make sense. But then God took me on a journey of discovery, which revealed that "success" looks different for every child and every family.

Though recurring themes surfaced, and those themes have been presented in this book, I was time and again reminded that *every* adoption story is unique and nuanced. There were insights and wisdom to be gained from each family I interviewed, and like all stories, theirs contained compelling characters and unique twists. One blanket statement can't possibly sum up the experience of any one of them. If I were to name what is perhaps the most important thing this journey has taught me, it's that adoption, like many things in life, is a land of paradox.

Parallel Realities

Recently I attended a retreat in Colorado for people leaving the mission field or overseas work assignments. The week was designed to give foreign workers and missionaries a safe space to process what it's like to move back "home" after living in another country for a significant period of time.

Surrounded by other Americans in a similar season of transition, our group talked about how, since returning to our homeland, we've found ourselves speaking in paradox and living parallel realities. As we processed what paradox meant in the context of our move from foreign to familiar, the facilitator helped us catch ourselves making statements that could be interpreted as contradictions:

"My life overseas was amazing, and I miss it."

"I was so lonely all the time."

"I couldn't get away from people!"

"I enjoyed getting to interact with so many new people."

"I missed Starbucks and convenience."

"I loved the access to so much fresh and organic food only a block from my apartment."

"Having to operate in another language every day was incredibly stressful."

"It was amazing how we were able to explore new places and converse with locals."

"I never truly fit in."

"It was exciting being the foreign anomaly wherever I went."

These statements may sound contradictory, but they're simply opposing thoughts that coexist simultaneously. All of them can be true for the person voicing what navigating a life between cultures is like. As our group of "misfit" Americans discussed the paradoxes we were experiencing as we readjusted to American life, it struck me that paradox is the best way to accurately summarize the adoption stories I'd been encountering for months.

Charles Dickens's classic, *A Tale of Two Cities*, famously begins with the quote, "It was the best of times, it was the worst of times."[1] I believe that many of the families you've encountered in this book live in the center of Dickens's statement. In saying yes to adoption, these families have experienced the highest of highs and the lowest of lows. As one father said, "It's the best thing we've ever done, and yet I would also say it's the hardest thing we've ever done."

It's part of the human condition to live in the midst of paradox, at the intersection of broken and beautiful. The challenge is learning that God can be found in conflicting realities. As one mother shared, "This whole adoption has reminded me that we are not called to be comfortable. We're meant to step outside of our comfort zone and make ourselves uncomfortable because that's where our growth is. Through our adoptions, we have been *really* uncomfortable. The irony is, I would say that being uncomfortable has also been oddly comforting."

Comfortably uncomfortable. To me this seems the perfect illustration of the paradox every adoptive family is living.

The Most Important Relationship

After I shared some of my findings with a colleague of mine who has provided counseling services for many adoptive families, he wrote me the following: "Thank you for being honest about what you experienced. Tampering with the most important relationship on earth always has a price. Both children and parents pay that price. And if you love, you hurt. It's a hard road, and it can be a burnout task."

I saved the email because something about that phrase, "the most important relationship on earth," struck a chord with me, and I knew I wanted to go back and give it more thought.

I've heard it said that adoption is not plan B. It's a nice phrase, but I don't know if it's inherently true. Perhaps for the parents it was never plan B, but I don't think we can say the same for the children. I believe God's original design was for children to be raised by their biological parents. His purpose was not for kids to be abandoned or born into situations of poverty that led to abuse, neglect, or substance addiction, only to be placed in an institution and perhaps adopted by another family.

But sin and human brokenness messed with that—with the *most important relationship on earth,* between parent and child. A relationship that was meant to reflect love and nurture became a casualty of sin. A relationship that was meant to point to the Fatherhood and provision of God instead left children fatherless and alone. That most important relationship was tampered with, and as a result, children have paid a heavy price. Adoptive parents have paid a heavy price. But as author Harville Hendrix famously said, "We are born in relationship, we are wounded in relationship, and we are healed in relationship." Nowhere have I seen this illustrated more clearly than in the arena of adoption.

I met with Jenna at a Starbucks about halfway through my trip. I vividly recall when Jenna and her husband, Dave, stayed in my home during the early years of my hospitality venture in Kyiv. They were first-time parents, had hosted their future daughter several times, and knew they were preparing to adopt a child with deep wounds. They'd done their homework. They took the classes, read the recommended books, had no other kids at home, and entered into adoption as trauma-informed as they could be. I remember thinking, "they've got this."

Over our lattes five years later, Jenna shared honestly about the struggles they encountered and the lessons God was teaching her.

"We went into this as people who knew the reality of adopting a kid with great needs and had an overwhelming desire to help. The irony is, my child does not want to be helped. She sees help as a weakness. Her life was so steeped in trauma. She has been in our home for many years, and, at seventeen, she still can't trust us. What I've realized is that I'm a fixer, but I can't fix her. As much as God is working in my life, I have to trust He'll work in her life."

She continued: "I've struggled with, 'Why is this happening? Why are there other families who haven't struggled nearly as much as we have?' It's hard not to be envious. But God is showing me this is more than just my daughter's story. This is a generational thing. You read in the Bible about generations that beget generations. You don't always see redemption on your timeline. I'm trying to hold on to hope. Sometimes I'm unsure, but I've learned I must stay in the fight, and I have to stay caring. I'm glad she's here with us, but it's very hard. I have to continually remind myself to keep God at the center of our story."

That afternoon with Jenna left a deep impression on me. We laughed as she shared humorous moments, and I was reminded of how learning to laugh at things helps families like Jenna's cope in the messy middle. We also cried as she shared about their struggles to reach a girl with multiple layers of trauma. We talked theory, and we talked faith, and we prayed for God to break through to her daughter. In Jenna I saw a woman wrestling with the paradoxes of her family's situation but also one with the spiritual maturity to resist lingering in the whys.

The Journey Continues

Like Susan in the previous chapter, Jenna is choosing to have faith that God is ultimately writing her family's story, and she realizes she doesn't have the vantage point to see how the story ends.

As I was writing this chapter, I was reminded that the stories of all those I interviewed are still being played out. Just yesterday I was reviewing the story of the pastor whose adopted son had received Christ but whose older adopted daughter was still wary of faith. She couldn't reconcile how a loving God would leave her in an orphanage until she was sixteen. Then today, I opened a message from the mother of that same young lady. It read:

> Julia called us last night wanting to talk. She wanted to receive Christ as her Savior. She said she sees how God has been directing her life, even in the bad parts when she was in an orphanage, and she now recognizes how He brought her into a good family, where she learned about the love of Jesus. She said the Lord had been tugging on her heart a lot lately and asked if she could be baptized right away. I always had a feeling the Lord would draw her to Himself after the long battle we went through to get her here. It's so sweet to see it becoming reality.

Sweet indeed. The day before, I'd reread a sentence about this girl's doubt and pain, and the next day I was hearing of her faith and healing!

About a year and a half after completing my road trip, I reached out to families I'd interviewed to inform them about my writing progress and to find out if they had any updates or addendums to their stories they'd like to share with me.

Recognizing that a lot could have transpired since sitting in their living rooms a year prior, I was curious to see if some of the families who'd been in the midst of a challenging season had seen any changes or breakthroughs.

As updates came in, some parents reported that things were relatively the same, with good and difficult days alike, and others reported discouragement over a child who seemed no closer to receiving help. But there were also encouraging emails that filled my inbox with hope and served as a reminder that God will never stop moving in the lives of adopted children and their families, bringing healing in His perfect time.

One adoptive mother, Meredith, wrote:

> We had a huge breakthrough when our daughter Emma shared some very heavy things she had been carrying. Emma, now twenty-two, has been a part of our family for six years, and we've seen her mature and grow in many incredible ways. However, until a few months ago, she'd always put up a strong barrier of anger and hesitation. Fortunately, that wall came crashing down and we were able to see our daughter begin to flourish and bloom for the first time. Up until this point, any offense, real or imagined, would trigger conflict and rejection for days. Things have now changed, and I'm incredibly thankful to the Lord. We have seen the good fruit that the power of God's presence can bring.

I want to add that I just returned from a ten-day vacation with my own adopted sister and two of our children. My sister was ten and I was eleven when she was adopted. She came to us with a history of severe trauma and abuse. At that time, we had no resources, help, or understanding, so as you can imagine, it went badly for many years. She is now a family therapist and helps many people. Even after all these years, God is still working to bring healing and hope to our relationship and knitting our families' hearts together. On our trip she was able to share things with me she'd been carrying for many years. It was a reminder that no matter how long, or what the timing is, God is always working to heal and bring us all to wholeness.

Another mother, Lucy, wrote, "When we last saw you, Misha had recently moved to another state, under difficult circumstances. We thank God for His grace in helping us to stay connected to Misha. We saw him in December, and then again in March, and began to rebuild our relationship with him. It was really awkward at first, but the Lord was with us. Misha was eager to come to our daughter's wedding last summer, so we bought him a plane ticket and met him there. It was a blessing and really significant, I believe, because it showed him that even though he messed up and there were consequences, we still love him and he's still part of the family."

Marta wrote me another encouraging story:

Since you sat at my table asking questions and listening to our story, a lot has happened. God has been healing hearts and restoring relationships. Our adopted son Daniel has made several visits to Ukraine in the past seven years. He visits his alcoholic mom and sister and tries to take care of them while he's there. He buys groceries and pays for electricity. His mom continues to drink too much even while he's visiting her, so he ends up cutting his time with her short.

Daniel returned to Ukraine this past October. As always, he visited his mom and sister and also his sister's kids. Her two little girls are with her ex-mother-in-law because the state may take them away from his sister. His sister had a premature baby boy last year. Because she drank and smoked during her pregnancy, the hospital could see the damage it caused, and she didn't get to take him home. He was put in an orphanage. Daniel finally came to understand that he can't change his biological relatives. He realized that nothing he could do or say would change the situation. He finally accepted that any change that happens can only come from them and God. It brought him freedom, and I think it also released him from any survivor's guilt.

When he returned from Ukraine, there was such a peace about him that even our other kids noticed it. We have seen so much healing in him and so much restoration between him and our other kids. We were all together on Christmas and there was no sabotage by Daniel. No drama. No arguing. No discomfort. No stress. It was amazing! We just keep praising God for all He is doing and all He has done.

God's Bigger Story

It's tempting to focus on the here and now and lose sight of a bigger picture. We have to keep in mind that our stories, and the stories of all the families described in this book, are part of a larger narrative.

An adoptive dad, Simon, shared his wisdom in relation to his two teens. "I am learning about Christ's love in a whole new way. I'm learning that love is about giving yourself constantly. I'm so much closer to the Lord now. More people know we are Christians now, and we're able to share our faith because of what we've gone through. People see that we chose a radical way to live, and even though we suck at it a lot of the time, they are seeing us persevere. Some people ask us, 'Why did you do this?' and we get to share why we did this. This whole thing is a window into God's love."

Another adoptive father shared about what the Lord was teaching him through the unresolved parts of their adoption journey. "The thing about fifty years of living is you realize there are always peaks and valleys in life. The good news about being in the valley is there is nowhere to go but up. I look back on our hardest moments with our son and I can say I grew more during those times than I grew when it was good."

In the face of unfinished or chaotic stories, I believe we come face-to-face with what we believe about God.

Do we know God? Or only things *about* God?

Do we *really* trust God? Or only offer lip service?

I wish I could say with confidence that all of the adoption stories I heard will be redeemed in a way worthy of a Hollywood movie. In the course of writing this book, however, I have been repeatedly challenged about my view of redemption and what it's "supposed" to look like. As discussed in previous chapters, from our Western perspective, a redemptive ending tends to mean happiness and resolution, on our terms. But recently I've been encouraged by the writing of Jerry Sittser in his book *A Grace Revealed*, where he looks at our life stories in light of God's bigger story. Sittser wrote:

> What can and should we expect from redemption? Will a Christian's story somehow read better than someone else's who doesn't believe in Christ's redemptive work? And what does "better" actually mean?
>
> . . . I want to say, redemption promises a happy ending, a kind of return to the garden, where all is goodness and happiness and bliss. I want to assure you that redemption means your lot in life is bound to improve, your circumstances will become more favorable. I want to call your story redemptive if,

after a painful divorce, you remarry again, this time
successfully; or if, after months of unemployment,
you land the ideal job; or if, after a period of sick-
ness, your child recovers and ends up competing in
the Olympics.

I would insert here a line for adoptive families: "Or if,
after adopting a child with a trauma background, you see
that child able to engage in healthy relationships and feel
completely bonded to your family."

Going back to the words of Sittser: "But all of this
assumes that favorable circumstances—remarriage, employ-
ment, health, success—capture the essence of redemption.
Then the question becomes, Is a positive outcome really the
point? Is happiness the proper goal? Is that what we should
expect of God?"[2]

In other words, How do we keep praising God when the
story doesn't always go the way we want it to go this side of
heaven? Will we grow weary and bitter? Or will we keep
pressing into who God is, even when our stories don't seem
to make sense?

Missionary and author Elisabeth Elliot once said,
"Things which sound like platitudes become vital, living and
powerful when you have to learn them in the bottom of the
barrel, in dark tunnels."[3] At times the adoption road can feel
more like a dark tunnel than an open road where we cruise
past corn fields under clear blue skies. But only in the dark
tunnel can any platitudes we have declared from ivory
towers be tested through the reality of our experiences.

More often than not, we can see what God is doing only when we look in the rearview mirror.

I remember back in high school being in a friend's vehicle where the rearview mirror had fallen off. He quickly discovered how often he needed it as he drove ahead. I had the job of holding up the mirror, and my arm soon felt the weight of providing the perspective he required to keep moving down the road. I learned a valuable lesson that day: seeing what's behind us is as important as seeing what's ahead of us. Yet there's a reason why the rearview mirror is small and the windshield is large. Where we are headed is more important than where we have been. We need the perspective of what's behind to guide us, but our focus needs to be on all that is yet to come.

As I traversed the United States, it was the views I saw in front of me or things I hoped to see that kept me moving forward—like the promise of experiencing my first New England autumn or the anticipation of viewing the immensity of the Grand Canyon. Some of the destinations on my list got checked off, others didn't, and there were numerous detours and surprises along the way. Such a parallel, I think, to the adoption experiences I documented.

I discovered that as families were given time to pause and look back, they gained perspective on how far they and their children had come. Even though the road before them remained uncertain, they could keep moving forward, knowing that the same God they could see in the rearview mirror would be with them around the next turn.

For Reflection or Group Discussion

1. Where have you seen growth in your own story? If you have adopted, what growth have you seen in your adopted child(ren) in the last six months?

2. What does the word *redemption* mean to you?

3. How do the stories in this chapter encourage you or give you hope?

Acknowledgements

After writing this book I now have a much greater understanding as to why people say "it takes a village!" This endeavor wouldn't have been possible without the many individuals who helped me along the way.

First and foremost, I would like to express my sincerest gratitude to the adoptive families who said yes to sharing their stories with me. You and your children are my heroes for the varying roads you have walked. Thank you for your honesty and vulnerability and for giving me a place to lay my often-weary head as I drove from city to city. I heard it said recently that hospitality is inviting people in as family in the hopes that they leave as friends. I can truly say that statement was proven true through all of you. Whether it was my home in Kyiv or yours in the US—I'm so grateful for the way our intersecting journeys united us as friends.

I am forever indebted to Terry Meeuwsen and Nataliya Khomyak, two women who had a God-sized vision and allowed me to be part of it. Terry and Nat, you both made this project possible. Thank you for not thinking I had a crazy idea but instead giving me your blessing to take on this cross-country adventure and book journey. I am forever grateful for your support and the support of the entire Orphan's Promise and CBN family. My story is inextricably linked to yours.

Jayne Schooler, thank you for your wisdom and early coaching in writing. I am so grateful for your helpful suggestions as I began, for being one of my greatest cheerleaders along the way, and for putting me in touch with the people I needed to make the book a reality.

Neva Wysong, thank you for being the first eyes to tackle my very first draft. I felt so safe in your hands! You believed in me and the words I had to share and helped craft and recraft so many sections to get the manuscript to the next level. Thank you for your brilliance in helping develop the chapter titles as well.

Traci Mullins, my brilliant and talented editor—I can't thank you enough for how you transformed my writing. You took my thoughts and helped put them in an order that made sense and crafted beauty out of my chaos. You have such a gift and I couldn't have done this without you.

Whitney Bak, my fabulous copy editor, thank you for seeing me to the finish line. To Cara Denney and Erin Friesen, thank you for being my final proof readers.

Ruby Johnston, I never would have guessed that a snowstorm in 2005 would be God's providential way of crossing our paths and uniting our lives. Your ideas, insight, and wisdom were so helpful to me as I crafted the questions I would ask families.

Nicole Wilke, whether you realize it or not, our one-hour Skype call in 2017 provided important guidance in how I would conduct and process my research in a manageable way. Your advice was invaluable, and every time I opened my highly detailed Excel spreadsheet, I said a silent thank-you to you for your helpful suggestions in how to categorize my findings.

To my GoFundMe me supporters who supplied the funding to make the road trip and the editing and printing of this book possible: thank you for believing in the importance of this project.

To Gwen Church, an adoptive mother who passed through my home many years ago and put a little thought in my head by simply saying, "You should write a book." I believe your words were the first seeds of this project.

Galina Schaefer, my faithful Ukrainian sidekick, your friendship and support both in work and life have been invaluable, and you have taught me servant leadership like no one else. Thank you for believing in me even when I have doubted myself. Я тебя люблю.

Olga Bulgakova, my beautiful producer and friend who created the film that helped raise the funds to make this project possible: your talent and artistry are a gift and your encouragement is a well that never runs dry. Спасибо тебе!

Tatiana Khrystynko—my first "boss" in Ukraine. You believed in twenty-five-year-old me when I felt out of my league, and you put me on a course that truly changed the direction of my life. I wouldn't be where I am today without your influence.

Steve and Kristi Weber—thank you for being my home away from home, my second parents, and for providing an opportunity in 2004 that changed the course of my life and, more importantly, changed *me*. I would never have come to Ukraine if it wasn't for your family, nor would I have stayed. I am eternally grateful to you for your love and support. Thank you for the countless kitchen table counseling sessions where we attempted to solve the world's problems over cups of coffee. You have been instrumental on every step of this journey.

To the cafés of Kyiv, for your endless supplies of affordable coffee while I spent hours typing in your corners. I especially appreciated the ones with quieter music and frequented you more often. I'm glad that the majority of these words were processed in the country where these stories were born.

Honnah Weber, my cousin and fabulous personal graphic designer—thank you for the stunning cover artwork you created and for all the creative beauty you pour into my life.

To my friends and family who joined me on the road and made those long driving days much more enjoyable, including Kris, Amber, Tara, Annamarie, Stacy, and Gabrielle—thank you for joining me on this journey!

To Richard, Heather, Caleb and Savvy, thank you for encouraging me to follow my dreams and write this book and for even flying to Arizona to cheer me on to the finish line. See, Caleb, you made it into your auntie's book after all!

To my parents, who released me into ministry many years ago when they let me fly away from home and then supported every endeavor along the way. Dad, I only wish you could have seen the completion of this project. Your driven, energetic spirit lives on and helped me keep pressing forward. Mom, thank you for being with me every step of the way, and for driving with me on this journey— whether that was when you were literally with me in the car or praying me through from a distance. You make life sweeter.

And, most importantly, to the Father, Son, and Holy Spirit. You are the Author of my story and of every story found in the pages of this book. Thank You for the journey You have taken me on and for being with me every step of the way. I am glad I know the Author of redemption who isn't finished with any of us yet.

Notes

Chapter Two

1 David Platt, *Radical* (Colorado Springs: Multnomah Books, 2010), 3.

2 "Orphans," UNICEF, https://www.unicef.org/media/orphans.

3 UNICEF, *Progress for Children: A Report Card on Child Protection (No. 8)*, September 2009, https://www.unicef.org/protection/Progress_for_Children-No.8_EN_081309(4).pdf.

4 Paulo Sérgio Pinheiro, *World Report on Violence Against Children*, UNICEF (Geneva: ATAR Roto Presse SA, 2006), https://www.unicef.org/violencestudy/I.%20World%20Report%20on%20Violence%20against%20Children.pdf.

5 *Children in Institutions: The Global Picture*, Better Care Network (Lumos, 2015), https://bettercarenetwork.org/sites/default/files/1.Global%20Numbers_2_0.pdf.

6 Ombudsman for Children with the president of Ukraine, *Building a Better Future for Children in Ukraine* (report), 2019.

7 Jason Bollinger, "Adoption Is Not the Gospel," *More Love to Give* (blog), May 13, 2015, https://morelovetogive.com/2015/05/13/adoption-is-not-the-gospel/.

229

Chapter Four

1 *Vulnerable Children in A Digital Age*, OVC Research (CAFO, 2019), 32, https://issuu.com/christianalliancefororphans/docs/e-book_with_links.

2 Association for Psychological Science, "Can Fetus Sense Mother's Psychological State? Study Suggests Yes," ScienceDaily, November 10, 2011, www.sciencedaily.com/releases/2011/11/ 1111101 42352.htm.

3 *Merck Manual*, Consumer Version, s.v. "Dehydration," https://www.merckmanuals.com/home/SearchResults?query=dehydration.

4 *Vulnerable Children in A Digital Age*, 32.

Chapter Seven

1 Jason Johnson, "The Real Enemy in Orphan Care," http://jasonjohnsonblog.com/blog/the-real-enemy-in-orphan-care#.Xjncgi3 Mw Wo=.

2 Loren Eiseley, *The Star Thrower* (New York: Times Books, 1978).

3 C. S. Lewis, preface to *The Screwtape Letters* (New York: Collier Books, 1961), ix.

4 Russell Moore, "Adoption's Formidable Enemy," Crossway, January 15, 2018, https://www.crossway.org/articles/adoptions-formidable-enemy/.

Chapter Nine

1 *Merriam-Webster*, s.v. "heal," https://www.merriam-webster.com/ dictionary/healing.

2 "TBRI®," Karyn Purvis Institute of Child Development, Texas Christian University College of Science & Engineering, https://child.tcu.edu/aboutus/tbri/#sthash.odnaDFKs.dpbs.

3 Fight or Flight Therapy, http://www.fightorflighttherapy.com.

4 Timothy J. Keller, "The Still Small Voice," sermon, Redeemer Presbyterian Church, September 26, 1999, New York, NY, MP3 audio, 14:30, https://gospelinlife.com/downloads/the-still-small-voice-8969/.

5 Keller, "The Still Small Voice," 18:15.

Chapter Ten

1 Jane Huang, reply to "How do you cut diamonds?" Quora, updated January 5, 2014, https://www.quora.com/How-do-you-cut-diamonds?no_redirect=1.

Chapter Eleven

1 Charles Dickens, *A Tale of Two Cities* (London: Chapman and Hall, 1859), 1.

2 Jerry Sittser, *A Grace Revealed* (Grand Rapids, MI: Zondervan, 2012), 77.

3 Elisabeth Elliot, "There's No Coming to Life without Pain: An Interview with Elisabeth Elliot," *Tabletalk*, Ligonier Ministries, February 1, 1989, https://www.ligonier.org/learn/articles/theres-no-coming-life-without-pain-interview-elisabeth-elliot/.